Glazing Techniques

Ceramic
Arts
Handbook
Series

Glazing Techniques

Edited by Anderson Turner
The American Ceramic Society
600 N. Cleveland Ave., Suite 210
Westerville, Ohio 43082
www.CeramicArtsDaily.org

The American Ceramic Society
600 N. Cleveland Ave., Suite 210
Westerville, OH 43082

© 2015 by The American Ceramic Society, All rights reserved.

ISBN: 978-1-57498-343-2 (Paperback)

ISBN: 978-1-57498-578-8 (PDF)

No part of this book may be reproduced, stored in a retrieval system or transmitted in any form or by any means, electronic, mechanical, photocopying, microfilming, recording or otherwise, without written permission from the publisher, except by a reviewer, who may quote brief passages in review.

Authorization to photocopy for internal or personal use beyond the limits of Sections 107 and 108 of the U.S. Copyright Law is granted by The American Ceramic Society, provided that the appropriate fee is paid directly to the Copyright Clearance Center, Inc., 222 Rosewood Drive, Danvers, MA 01923 U.S.A., www.copyright.com. Prior to photocopying items for educational classroom use, please contact Copyright Clearance Center, Inc. This consent does not extend to copyright items for general distribution or for advertising or promotional purposes or to republishing items in whole or in part in any work in any format. Requests for special photocopying permission and reprint requests should be directed to Director, Publications, The American Ceramic Society, 600 N. Cleveland Ave., Westerville, Ohio 43082 USA.

Every effort has been made to ensure that all the information in this book is accurate. Due to differing conditions, equipment, tools, and individual skills, the publisher cannot be responsible for any injuries, losses, and other damages that may result from the use of the information in this book. Final determination of the suitability of any information, procedure or product for use contemplated by any user, and the manner of that use, is the sole responsibility of the user. This book is intended for informational purposes only.

The views, opinions and findings contained in this book are those of the author. The publishers, editors, reviewers and author assume no responsibility or liability for errors or any consequences arising from the use of the information contained herein. Registered names and trademarks, etc., used in this publication, even without specific indication thereof, are not to be considered unprotected by the law. Mention of trade names of commercial products does not constitute endorsement or recommendation for use by the publishers, editors or authors.

Publisher: Charles Spahr, Executive Director, The American Ceramic Society

Managing Director: Sherman Hall

Editor: Bill Jones

Graphic Production: Pamela S. Woodworth

Series Design: Melissa Bury

Cover Image: Cups by Adero Willard

Frontispiece: *Tall Ewer: Grey with Fruit*, by Linda Arbuckle

Table of Contents

1 Basic Techniques and Tools

Creative Commercial Glazing   1
Deanna Ranlett

Glazing for Success   5
Annie Chrietzberg

Using the Correct Brush   9
Michael Harbridge

Making Brushes   11
David L. Gamble

How to Use a Spray Gun   15
Roger Graham

Spraying Glazes   21
Kathy Chamberlin

Resists Review   24
Deanna Ranlett

Glaze Drip Pan   27
Jim Wylder

2 Graphic Pattern and Imagery

Vinyl Stencils   29
Jay Jensen

Stay-Put Stencils   31
Roger Graham

Projecting a Pattern   34
Shana Angela Salaff

Pouncing and Coloring Patterns   36
Susan Mussi

Creating Geometric Patterns   38
Anthony Merino with Pam Luke

Less is More   42
Courtney Murphy

Slip and Sgraffito   45
Kristin Pavelka

Pennsylvania Redware   48
Denise Wilz

Black on White Mimbres Decoration   52
Tracy Gamble

Majolica Imagery   55
Jake Allee

Glazing Patterns   58
Frank James Fisher

Poured Decoration   61
Sam Scott

Sarah Jaeger's Botanical Patterns   63
Emily Donahoe

Fumiya Mukoyama's Zogan Yusai   66
Naomi Tsukamoto

3 Creating Layers and Depth

Using Gravity to Enhance a Surface   71
Kari E. Radasch

Layered Decoration   73
Adero Willard

Combining Clay, Stain and Glaze   80
Marty Fielding

Watercolor Maiolica   82
Laurie Curtis

Stains, Slips and Patience *Scott Ziegler*		87
Adding Depth to Your Glazes *Lisa Bare Culp*		89
Textile Inspired Designs *Colleen Riley*		92
Hunt Prothro's Stains and Underglazes *Susan Chappelear*		96

4 Specialized Techniques

Low-Fire Electric Reds *David L. Gamble*	99
Mastering Mica *Kate and Will Jacobson*	102
The Colorful World of Majolica *Linda Arbuckle*	105
Majolica with Lusters *Liz Quackenbush*	110
The Majolica of Posey Bacopoulos *Clay Cunningham*	113
China Painting Basics *Paul Lewing*	119
Using Lusters *Jonathan Kaplan*	123
Combining Fired and Post-Fired Surfaces *Magda Gluszek*	127
Aged Patina *Philippe Faraut*	131
Working with Soluble Salts *Diane Chin Lui*	133

Preface

A long time ago, a friend who was a gallery director shared with me the insight that, "We make art for our friends." I take this to mean that we make art that has meaning to our peer group and colleagues. That meaning can have something to do with subject matter or content, but it can just as easily have something to do with craftsmanship, finish, or in the case of ceramics—glaze. Through the last fifty years of studio ceramics that peer-to-peer sharing has helped to create a bevy of technical knowledge that grows a little bit every day.

We have so many options in glazing today. Even though the mystery of what happens in the kiln has long since gone by the wayside, glaze is still hard for many of us to conquer. Too often an artist makes a poor glaze choice when a quality choice was within their reach.

It's as if we forget all of our training and go crazy with color. Or perhaps we reject color and forget how it can assist in meaning, dimension and the overall spirit of a piece. Our process in clay does not end with the forming of an object. In order to connect with others or our peers, we must consider all aspects including glaze; or our work, unfortunately, will have a difficult time transcending time and obtainig a life of it's own to share with friends yet to come.

This book contains information on all aspects of glazing from the simple to the complex and highly technical. We've included the research of several different artists that I hope will inform and inspire you to reach and discover more about glaze on your own.

Anderson Turner

1

Basic Techniques and Tools
CREATIVE COMMERCIAL GLAZING

by Deanna Ranlett

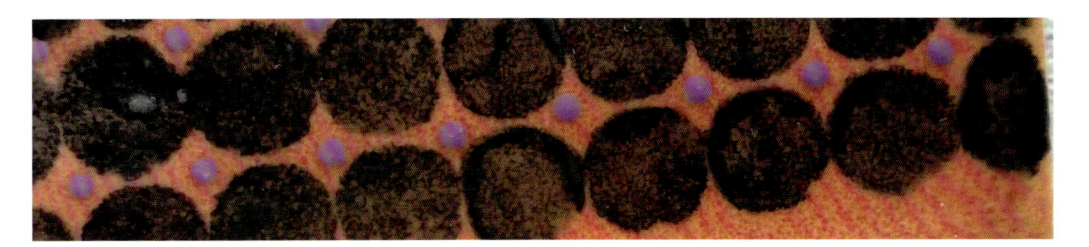

I often find there is a stigma surrounding using commercial glazes or a lack of confidence about what they can do beyond what the directions say. It's important to remember that the directions are a general guideline, this means that you'll need to test for success even with commercial products. Just because a jar says three coats of a glaze are needed, that doesn't mean two, four, or even five coats might not work better for you.

When using commercial products, many people struggle with the idea that their piece might look exactly like someone else's who bought the same product. Others say they have trouble applying them in ways they like or that the glazes don't look like the test tile. But hey, that's why you have to test them on your clay body and in your kiln! Don't just crack open a jar and expect perfection.

So, how do you make them your own? I experimented with wax resist, stencils, paper resist, and underglaze to change the way the commercial glazes are commonly applied. This led to a lot of new ways to use the commercial glazes I already had in my studio.

What's in the Jar

Here's what commercial glazes have going for them:
- Teams of researchers and testers have already worked out the kinks.
- A brand's glaze line tends to be very compatible for layering, and using in combination with multiple techniques.
- Extra binders, brushing mediums, and additives are added to help adhesion, application, and even drying.
- Commercial glazes are very smooth—they've been ball-milled, sieved, and mixed better than we're capable of in our own studios.
- Many glazes have a wider range than the directions indicate—low-fire products can often fire up to cone 6.

Preparation and Application

Always prepare the ceramic piece you want to apply commercial glazes to by bisque firing it first to cone 04—a hotter bisque firing drives off organic materials that can cause problems in the glaze firing and makes the ceramic slightly less porous. I also wipe it down with a damp sponge to make sure it's free of oil and dust.

You can apply commercial glazes by pouring, dipping, or spraying, and you can also adjust their thinness or thickness depending on your needs. Commercial glazes can also be brushed on using anything from a hake or fan brush for wide coverage to a soft script liner if you're doing detail work. Remember that colors could mix during the firing, so what you see in the jar might not always be what you get when you open the kiln. For example, brushing purple over green might make the purple appear more brown than you expected.

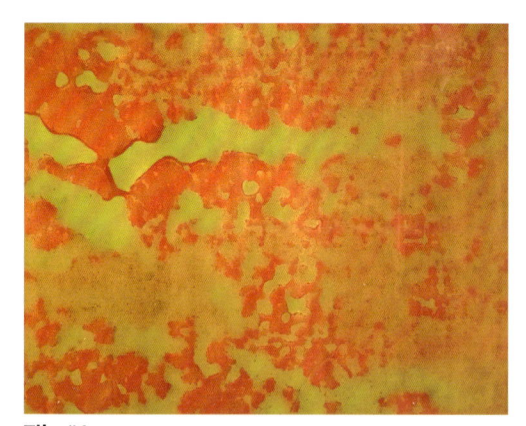

Tile #1

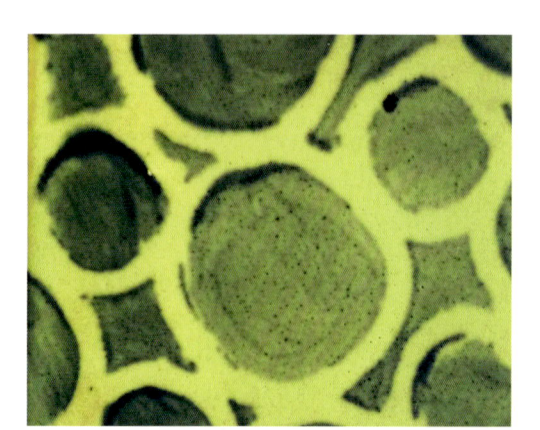

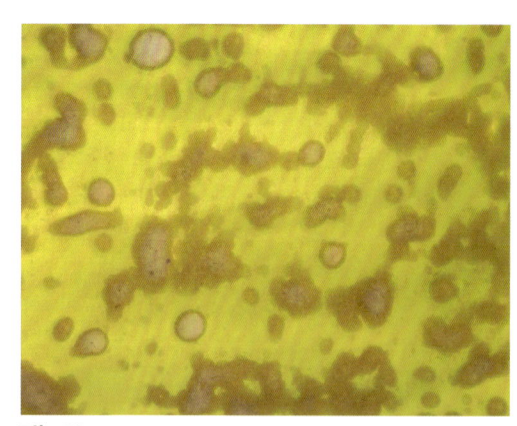

Tile #2

Tile #3

Tile #4

Wax Resist Combinations

We've all used wax resist on bisqueware before glazing, but you can also combine it with commercial glazes for dramatic results.

Tile #1: I started by brushing on two coats of Mayco Foundations Deep Red FN-035 glaze and allowed it to dry, then I sprayed wax resist over it using a hairspray atomizer and allowed it to dry. Next, I brushed a coat of Mayco Foundations Green FN-007 glaze on the tile and let it bead up. After the green glaze dried, I mixed together a small amount of Mayco Stroke & Coat SC-6 Sunkissed (yellow) with a small amount of Forbes wax directly together (DON'T do this in your glaze jar). I brushed this mixture over the whole tile and fired it to cone 05. The green fully melted into the red and created a lovely orange effect.

Tile #2: I brushed two coats of Mayco Foundations Green FN-007 glaze, then sprayed wax super close to the tile and allowed it to dry. Next, I took ½ cup of Amaco Clear Transparent LG-10 glaze tinted with 1 teaspoon of PSH (The Pottery Supply House) Lilac underglaze and applied a single coat over the top then fired it to cone 05.

Stencil Applications

Pre-cut stencils can be taped to a flat or curved surface using blue painters tape to achieve multiple layers of decoration with commercial glazes. This technique provides a ton of visual interest with endless possibilities for exploration.

Tile #3: I brushed one coat of Mayco Stoneware Glaze Mirror Black, then taped a pre-cut stencil over the dried surface, and applied two coats of Mayco Stoneware Glaze Green Opal. The opal is very nice over the black because the black has

Basic Techniques and Tools

Tile #5

Tile #6

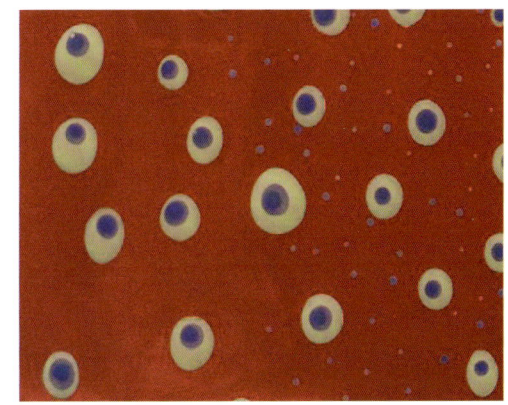

Tile #7

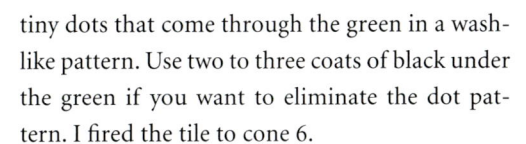

Tile #8

tiny dots that come through the green in a wash-like pattern. Use two to three coats of black under the green if you want to eliminate the dot pattern. I fired the tile to cone 6.

Tile #4: I brushed one coat of Mayco Foundations White FN-001 glaze over a single layer of Mayco Foundations Green FN-007 glaze in a striped pattern. I then used stencils to sponge on decorative shapes in a transparent purple glaze (from the recipe in tile #2). To add definition, I waxed over the flags in a cloud-shaped pattern then carved through them using a fine-tipped needle tool. Finally, I rubbed Amaco Black LUG-1 underglaze into the sketched lines and wiped off any extra black lying on the surface outside the lines. I fired the tile to cone 05.

Tile #5: I applied two coats of Mayco Foundations Green FN-007 glaze. While the second coat was damp, I adhered paper circles onto the surface. Then, I applied a third coat of the Mayco Foundations Green FN-007 glaze. When that dried, I dry–brushed Mayco Stroke & Coat SC-88 TuTu Tango (coral) glaze over the top of the entire tile. Finally, I slip trailed tiny purple dots using PSH Lilac underglaze around the stencils. When those dried I removed the stencils and fired the tile to cone 05.

Screen Printing and Slip Trailing Ideas

Tile #6: I screen-printed Amaco LUG-1 black underglaze patterns and slip trailed drawings using Mayco Designer Liner Black SG-401 glaze. Then I slip trailed a small amount of transparent PSH Lilac underglaze mixed with Amaco Clear Transparent LG-10 glaze to create faux drips running down the tile even though it was fired flat to cone 05.

Tile #7: I screen-printed Amaco LUG-1 black

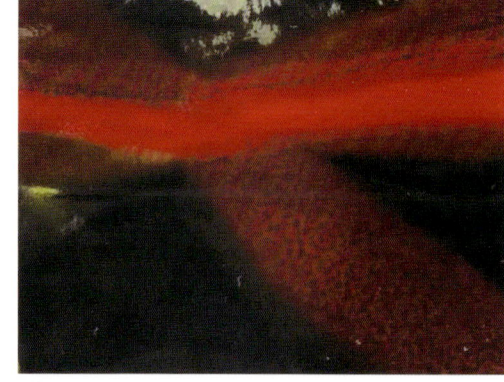

Tile #9

Tile #10

Tile #11

Tile #12

underglaze patterns, drew with Mayco Designer Liner Black SG-401 glaze, then coated the drawings with three coats of Mayco SW-201 Turquoise glaze before firing the tile to cone 6.

Tile #8: I applied three coats of Mayco Foundations Deep Red FN-035, then slip trailed dots of Mayco Foundations Tan glaze FN-022. While those were still wet, I applied PSH Lilac underglaze over the tan dots and fired the tile to cone 05.

Tile #9: I brushed three coats of Amaco Celebration Amethyst HF-171 glaze over the full tile, then slip trailed a beehive pattern with Mayco Designer Liner Black SG-401 glaze on top, and fired it to cone 05.

Layering Effects

Tile #10: I applied a base coat of Mayco Stoneware Glaze Mirror Black then brushed Mayco Stroke & Coat SC-74 Hot Tamale (red) on top in an X pattern and fired it to cone 6. The glazes mottled depending on the amount of glaze on the brush and the weight of the stroke.

Tile #11: Two coats each of Amaco Celebration Amethyst HF-171 glaze and Mayco Stoneware Glaze Mirror Black were brushed on in a stripe pattern. Then two coats of Mayco Turquoise SW-201 were brushed on top of that before the tile was fired to cone 6.

Tile #12: I brushed one coat of Mayco Foundations Deep Red FN-035 mixed with Mayco Stroke & Coat SC-6 Sunkissed (yellow). Then I brushed on one coat of the Sunkissed glaze/wax mixture. Finally, I screen printed a coat of Amaco Black LUG-1 underglaze on top and made purple dots with a slip trailer using PSH Lilac Underglaze. The tile was fired to cone 6.

Basic Techniques and Tools
GLAZING FOR SUCCESS

by Annie Chrietzberg

For a lot of people glazing is the bane of their ceramic lives. While there's no specific glazing system that fits everyone's needs and preferences, the more information you have allows you more options when you get into a glazing corner. My system for glazing evolved with my own body of work, and as the work changes, I draw on various aspects of it to suit the particulars of the pieces in front of me.

For complex forms consisting of thrown and textured elements, I use a combination of pouring, dipping and brushing to get the color where I want it. Dipping is the easiest way to ensure an even application, and pouring, with a little practice, is the next. Brushing takes more practice, time and attention, and I only use it when the first two methods are not options for a tricky place on a pot.

The two troublemakers involved with glaze application are water and gravity. When a bisque pot becomes too saturated with water, it won't accept glaze correctly, so use the least amount of water possible when glazing, including when you are making corrections. And as for gravity, I doubt there's anyone who hasn't experienced the wayward drip of one glaze flowing toward the earth across the perfect application of the previous glaze.

Tips for Success

- Keep bisqueware clean. Lotions, or even the oils from your hands, can create resist spots where glaze adheres unevenly or not at all. Throughout all phases of the glazing process, including load-

Glazing complicated pieces requires pouring, dipping and brushing of glazes. Practicing with various techniques ensures greater success with each piece you complete.

ing and unloading the kiln, handle bisqueware with a clean pair of disposable gloves (figure 1). If you think your bisqueware has been compromised—splashed with something, covered with grime, or maybe handled by a visitor—bisque it again rather than risk a crawling glaze.
- Remove all dust before glazing including bisque dust, studio dust and even household or street dust. Use an air compressor for foolproof results, but work outside or in a well-ventilated area away from your primary workspace, as bisque dust is extremely abrasive to your lungs (figure 2).
- Use silicon carbide paper to remove any rough spots you missed before bisque firing. Place your work on a piece of foam to prevent chipping. After sanding, wipe with a damp sponge to remove all traces of sanding dust (figure 3).

Glazing Techniques

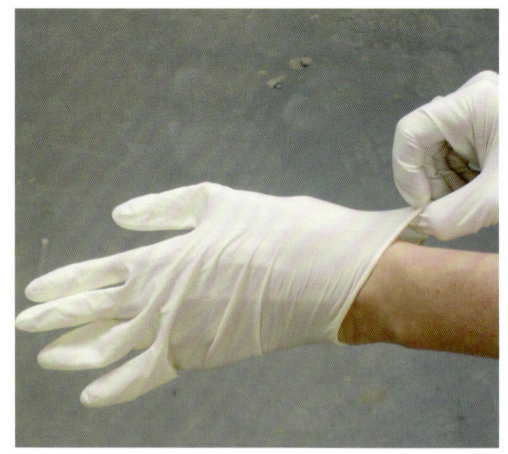

1. Keep bisqueware clean by handling bisqueware with a clean pair of disposable gloves.

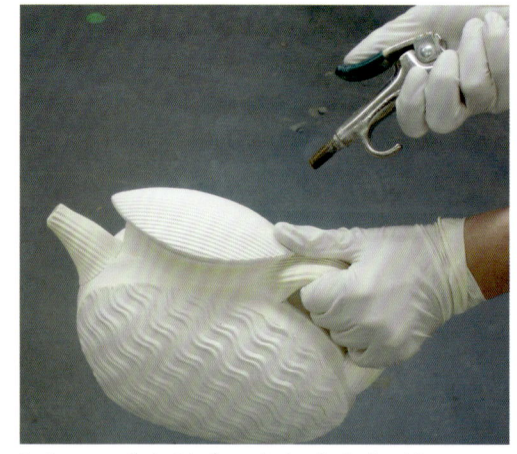

2. Remove all dust before glazing including bisque dust, studio dust and even household or street dust.

3. Use silicon carbide paper to remove any rough spots you missed before bisque firing.

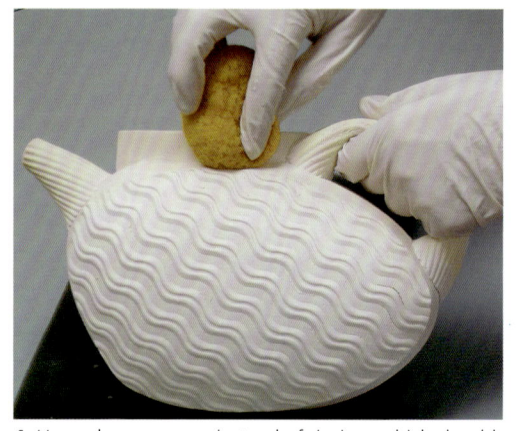

4. Use a damp sponge instead of rinsing, which should be kept to a minimum.

- Use a damp sponge instead of rinsing, which should be kept to a minimum. Wring the sponge thoroughly and rotate it so each area is only used once. I tend to use half a dozen or so of those orange round synthetic sponges during any given glazing session (figure 4).
- Glazes must be well mixed and I use an electric drill with a Jiffy Mixer attached (figure 5). If there is dry glaze caked on the sides of the bucket, sieve the glaze, then return it to a clean bucket.
- Glaze all the interiors of your pots first by pouring the glaze in, then rolling it around for complete coverage. For complex pieces requiring a number of glazing steps, glaze the insides the day before to give you a drier surface to work with, especially for brushing (figure 6).
- When removing unwanted glaze, scrape off as much of it as you can with a dental tool or a similar small metal scraper to keep a sharp line. A damp sponge removes the remaining glaze with a few strokes, keeping water usage to a minimum (figure 7).
- Use a stiff brush to help clean glaze drips out of texture (figure 8).
- For dipping glazes, select an appropriately sized container for the work at hand. I have lots of different sizes of shallow bowls that are perfect for dipping the sides of my pieces. Wide shallow bowls allow me to see what I'm doing,

Basic Techniques and Tools

5. For best results, use an electric drill with a Jiffy Mixer attached to assure glazes are well-mixed.

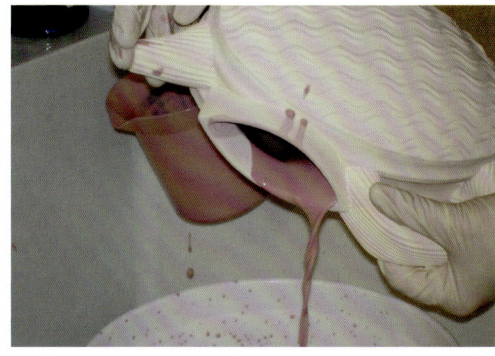

6. Glaze all the interiors of your pots first by pouring the glaze in, then rolling it around for complete coverage.

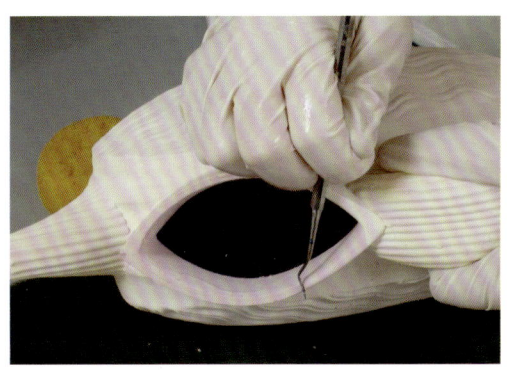

7. Remove remaining glaze with a few strokes of a sponge, keeping water usage to a minimum.

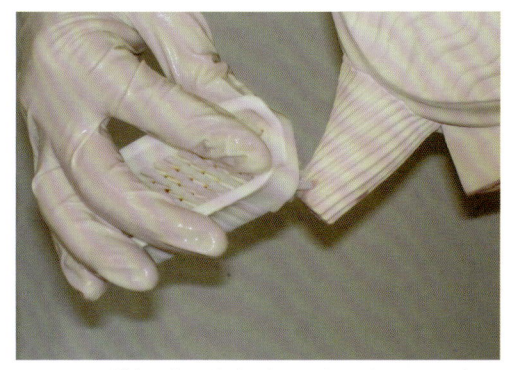

8. Use a stiff brush to help clean glaze drips out of the texture.

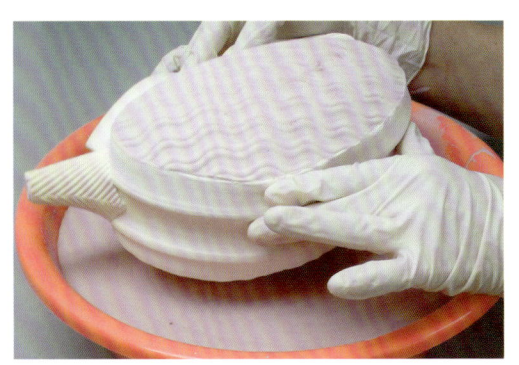

9. For dipping glazes, select an appropriately sized container for the work at hand.

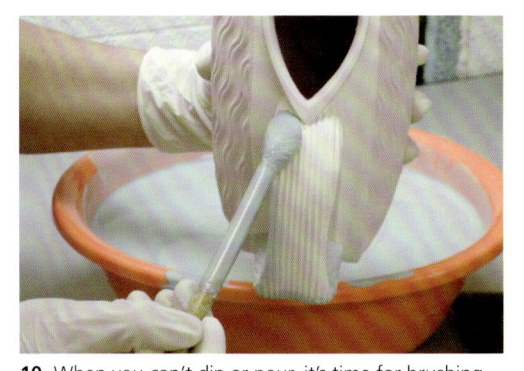

10. When you can't dip or pour, it's time for brushing.

so I even use them for smaller things that fit into the glaze bucket (figure 9).

- When you can't dip or pour, it's time for brushing. Watch your bisque as you brush—glaze is shiny and wet when first applied, then becomes matt as the bisque absorbs the water. If you re-coat too soon over a damp coat, you'll move the foundation layer rather than imparting a second coat (figure 10).
- Consider gravity when brushing and hold the pot both to encourage the glaze to go where you want it to and to keep it from running where you don't want it (figure 11).
- If a drip flows onto a previously glazed surface,

Glazing Techniques

11. Hold the pot both to keep glaze from running where you don't want it.

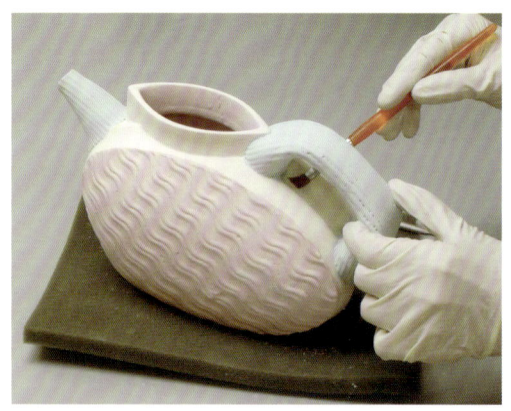

12. Use a small compact brush to wipe away glaze in areas you can't reach with a sponge.

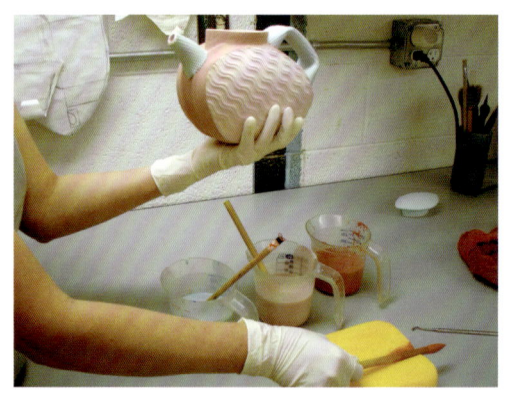

13. Keep a large, damp sponge nearby to keep the brush handle clean.

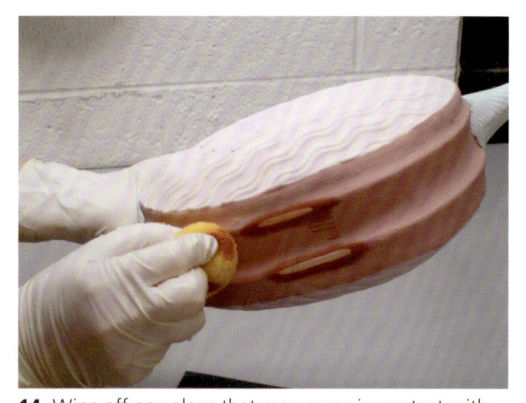

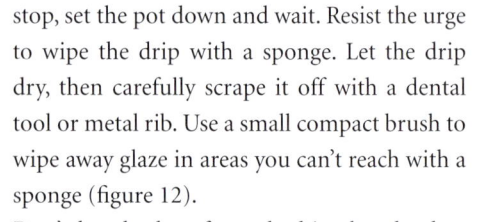

14. Wipe off any glaze that may come in contact with the kiln shelf.

stop, set the pot down and wait. Resist the urge to wipe the drip with a sponge. Let the drip dry, then carefully scrape it off with a dental tool or metal rib. Use a small compact brush to wipe away glaze in areas you can't reach with a sponge (figure 12).

- Don't brush glaze from the big glaze bucket. Pour a small amount into a cup, then briskly stir it occasionally to ensure that it stays properly mixed. Keep a large, damp sponge nearby to keep the brush handle clean. Stray drips often start with a handle full of glaze (figure 13).
- If you're glazing pots that don't have a defined foot, push them across a piece of 220-grit silicon carbide sandpaper. The sandpaper removes some of the glaze from the contact areas, indicating where you need to wipe off the remaining glaze (figure 14).

Brushes

I use sumi brushes, which have long bristles that come to a point, but I have also used hake and multi-stemmed hake brushes for large areas. Mop brushes might work for you, but don't buy expensive watercolor brushes. Applying glaze is a cruder application than watercolor, and an expensive, fine watercolor brush won't work as well for a glaze as a cheap hake from the ceramic supply store.

A brush with long, springy bristles that come to a point is best. Successful brushing not only relies on technique of application, but also the glazes you're using and the temperature you're firing to. Some glazes lend themselves well to brushing, while others are more finicky. Make wide tiles representative of your surfaces and use them to test how well your glazes take to brushing.

Basic Techniques and Tools
USING THE CORRECT BRUSH

by Michael Harbridge

You can spend a great deal of time creating unique shapes only to suffer disappointment with the final project because the glaze finish comes out streaky or blotchy. Selecting the proper brush is an important part of the creative process and knowing what to look for in a brush can alleviate frustration.

With literally thousands of different brushes on the market in a variety of sizes, styles, and hair types, where do you begin to narrow the search? While the pack of large brushes from the dollar store may be appealing from the price standpoint, it may not be the best option. The kind of hair, shape, and length of the bristle will have a dramatic effect on the final outcome.

Brush Hair

In most cases, soft bristles are the preference when applying engobes, ceramic colorants and glazes. If a bristle is too stiff, it will drag, spreading colors or glazes too thin. You'll generally find three different kinds of bristle options. Synthetic hair is a manufactured product often made of nylon and can have a plastic feel. The thickness of the bristle will make a big difference in how well the brush performs. Many inexpensive brushes have thick, stiff plastic bristles. These brushes will not hold or apply color well. The rough, jagged ends of the hairs will likely leave streaks in the colors. Quality synthetics have finer hair, are much softer and the bristles come to a nice point.

Natural hair brushes are usually the best option for glazing. However, not all types of natural hair brushes will work. While hog bristle brushes are made with natural hairs, these stiff, white hairs are not the best option for glazing. Goat hair is also a white bristle but has a plush, soft feel and is a favorite for many artists. Badger hair and blends of soft hair like squirrel also make fine brushes for use with engobes and glazes. The final type is a blend of natural and synthetic bristles. These brushes vary, depending upon the combination of hairs. Some natural bristles are soft and limp when loaded with glaze. By adding some firmer synthetic or natural bristles within the soft hairs, the brush can hold its shape better and give nice coverage.

Shape and Size

You may not think the shape of a brush would make a difference. Pick up a fan brush and a flat brush with the same hair and run your fingers across the bristles. The bristles in the flat brush are probably packed tighter and have a shorter length. Even though the hair is the same, the fan will lay the color on better. Will a #2 flat perform differently than a #12 flat? Absolutely! The numbers on brushes refer to the size, with numbers increasing as the brush size increases. Many artists use a larger brush on the main area and a smaller version of the same brush to go around details. It's possible they'll get streaks or starved glaze areas where the smaller brush is used because the brush doesn't hold as much color and it requires more frequent loading. The artist is also making many more short strokes rather than long, gliding motions.

Glazing Techniques

Left: Stiff fan brush. One coat of glaze applied with this stiff, natural hog hair bristle, fan shaped brush left a streaky finish.

Right: Badger hair fan brush. Badger hair holds lots of color and does a great job of depositing smooth layers of color. One coat of glaze applied using this brush gave good coverage and had less texture.

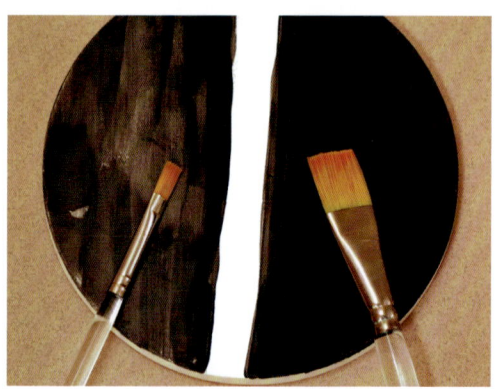

Left: Small flat synthetic brush. While these synthetic brushes have soft bristles, the small size and tightly bound hairs don't hold as much color as a fan and require more frequent loading. One coat of glaze came out streaky.

Right: Large flat synthetic brush. The larger size of this brush helped give a little better coverage than the smaller version on the right.

Left: Soft goat hair hake brush. Hake brushes are ideal for glazing and come in a variety of sizes. The soft hair holds a lot of glaze and layers nicely.

Right: Dollar store synthetic brush. This inexpensive brush has thick plastic bristles. It was difficult to get this brush to cover the surface with glaze because the coarse hairs scraped and dragged the color, leaving a very streaky finish.

It's always best to use the largest brush possible. If a smaller brush is required for fine work areas, watch to be sure the brush is being loaded well and the colors or glazes are being applied evenly. Brushes like the hake and soft fans are ideal for covering large areas. They usually lay the color or glaze on well without dragging through and creating streaks.

Stiffer fans are perfect for textured or thick engobes, colorants, and glazes because they require a brush capable of lifting and holding the products.

Soft goat hair fans are too limp and will have a difficult time picking up thick or textured glazes and spreading them evenly. Stiffer brushes also reach down into highly textured or detailed spots. It may work best to apply the first coat on textured items with a stiff fan and apply subsequent coats with a softer brush. Using a stiff brush for all coats could result in the colors filling in the crevices, while actually dragging and pulling the color from the high points or tips of the texture, leaving a starved area.

Basic Techniques and Tools
MAKING BRUSHES

by David L. Gamble

From left to right: Gray squirrel, deer (natural), deer (dyed red), and red squirrel.

Your surface decoration is one of a kind. So why not make brushes customized to exactly fit your techniques and style?

Using the right tool for the job is always a good idea, but in ceramics, using the right brush is critical for creating certain marks on your pots. You'd have a difficult time trying to use a short flat brush to create a long thin line, yet when using the right brush, you can create that line without any effort at all.

Brushes are made from a wide variety of either animal hair or synthetics. The material affects how the brush loads and disperses a medium. For example, red sable hair is the best choice for watercolors and washes even though less expensive brushes can be made from camel, squirrel or horse hair. Stiff boar or hog bristles are good for oil paint, while in ceramics we tend to use hairs that load a lot of glaze, so we choose goat and china bristles (the industry term for hog hair). China bristles are normally longer and stiffer than goat hair.

By making your own brushes, you can control the qualities that are unique to you. Though manufactured brushes are made to perform well with certain media, as artists we tend to use whatever will work to make the marks we want.

I've been constructing brushes on and off for many decades, and have presented workshops over the years, first along with potter Steve Howell, and most recently with my wife Tracy who is also a ceramic artist. We have participants make brushes on the first day of our two-day presentations, and use them on the second day. During one demonstration at Atlantic Pottery in Florida last year, Bob Kirk, a high school art teacher, was demonstrating making brushes and told me he has made brushes in classes with his students. I think that everyone from students (at all levels) to seasoned artists can appreciate the quality of a good brush after spending the time making their own.

Glazing Techniques

Materials List

- Bamboo: Select pieces ¼–½ inches in diameter. There are more than 1450 species with 450 species sold in the US, so there's a wide variety available! If you cut fresh bamboo, allow it to dry for a month before using for handles.
- Hair: I've found that deer and squirrel tail hair work well to hold and disperse the glaze. Squirrel and deer tails can be purchased at any fishing store that sells fly fishing materials to tie flies. Deer tail is packaged natural and in a variety of bright colors to imitate the color of insects. Also try dog, skunk, elk, fox, goat, etc. Note: Human hair is too limp to use.
- Dental floss: Use strong dental floss to tie the hairs together. Waxed dental floss is a bit more sticky and easier to tie. Non-waxed dental floss is a bit harder to tie but accepts the glue better. I prefer the waxed dental floss.
- Masking tape
- Sandpaper
- Hacksaw with fine blade
- White glue
- Needle tool
- Small drill bit ($1/8$–$5/32$ inch in diameter)
- Cotton thread/string

Process

To begin making your brush, select the hair you're going to use and get an extra long piece of dental floss to wrap the bottom of the hairs. Four hands work best for this so get someone to hold the hairs as you tie them (figure 1). Do not trim the floss yet. Next, cut the hairs at the base. Start with at least one inch of hair. If you want a longer brush, deer tail hair can be 3–4 inches in length or longer if you use most of the tail. Remember that you'll need to leave about ¼- to ½-inch of hair to glue and wrap together (figure 2), so if you want a 1-inch-long brush tip, cut the hair to 1½ inches. Dip the cut end of the brush hair into a puddle of white glue (figure 3). Allow the hair to soak up the glue. Wrap and tightly tie the rest of the floss, forcing the base of the hairs together into a tightly bound tube-like shape (figure 4). Allow to dry before gluing into the handle.

Choose a piece of bamboo that your brush hair will fit into tightly. Hold the bamboo behind a node like a brush to make sure it's comfortable. Bamboo is hollow between the nodes so decide how long you want the handle, and leave about ¾ of an inch before you reach the node to create a natural ferrule you can fill with glue.

Wrap masking tape around the end of the bamboo where you plan to cut and use a fine-toothed hacksaw or jeweler's saw to cut the bamboo (figure 5). The tape keeps the bamboo from splintering. Sand both ends smooth (figure 6).

1. Tie the base of the hair with floss.

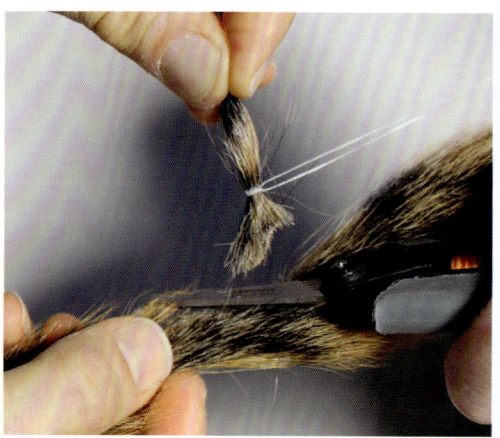

2. Trim the hairs at the base.

Basic Techniques and Tools

3. Dip the cut end in glue.

4. Wrap and tightly tie the rest of the floss.

5. Cut bamboo with a fine tooth saw.

6. Sand both handle ends smooth.

7. Test fit the brush then add glue.

8. Insert brush then use a needle tool to shove it in tight.

Test fit the brush hair in the handle then fill the ferrule space with glue (figure 7) and force the brush hair into it. Use a needle tool to shove it in tight so that the dental floss wrapping cannot be seen (figure 8). Let it dry.

Drill a hole through the bamboo at the end of the handle using a small drill bit so you can add a thread to hang the brush up (figure 9). You can also sand flat a section at the top of the handle so you can write your name on the brush with a permanent marker. Tung oil can be used on the handle for a finishing touch. No other finishing or waterproofing is needed. Over time, the oils from your hand will give the brush handle a nice patina.

13

Glazing Techniques

9. Drill a hole in the top of the handle for hanging.

10. Split the bamboo end with a knife.

11. Wrap with thread creating a loop with the beginning of the thread and wrapping around it to secure.

12. Put the end of the thread through the loop and pull the bottom end down to pull the end through.

As an alternative, you can also split the bamboo ferrule with an X-Acto knife deep enough for the brush hair to fit in (figure 10). This works well if the opening in the bamboo is a bit too small for the brush hair to fit in. Place glue inside and insert the brush hair. Wrap the end tightly (figure 11) then place the end of the thread through the loop you have left at the top and pull the bottom thread until the end is pulled into the wrapping (figure 12). Trim off excess thread and add a thin amount of white glue over the wrap. I've also heard of thin copper wire being used.

With either method, once you've secured the brush hairs into the ferrule and the glue has dried, thread a piece of ribbon, twine, string or a leather strap through the hole at the end to create a hanging loop (figure 13). This finishing touch is just one more way to create your own special brushes.

13. Thread a cord for hanging the brushes through the hole drilled at the end of the handle.

Basic Techniques and Tools
HOW TO USE A SPRAY GUN

by Roger Graham

Spray-glazed platter. The gradation in tone from the center to the rim would be hard to create if the glaze was applied any other way.

While a lot of pottery textbooks discuss glaze spraying, coverage is often sparse, but spray glaze application has a lot going for it if you do it right. Spraying glazes allows you to save on material costs, as you can even glaze large forms with a small amount of glaze. Since you can mix smaller quantities of glaze, you'll have room in your studio to store (and therefore experiment with) a wider variety of glazes. Once you are familiar with the thickness of the sprayed glaze that gives you the result you want, you can repeat the results easily, and calculate how much glaze you'll need to use for any standard forms you make.

Choosing a Spray Gun

There are different options when choosing a spray gun. You'll need to consider how many pots you usually glaze at a time, and how often you plan to switch between colors. Beyond this, you'll also need to consider space requirements—room for a compressor and spray booth if your spraying will take place inside.

The most common kind of spray gun is called a suction-feed gun. It has a container or pot beneath it to hold the liquid, and it is intended for paint spraying, where you expect to use a pint of paint between refills (figure 1). This is the kind often shown in the illustration in a textbook. It's better than no gun at all, but for spraying glaze on pottery, there is a better choice, a gravity-feed spray gun (figure 2). These are usually smaller in size, intended for holding only a small quantity of liquid, and easy to wash out. The container is located on top of the gun and fluid drains into the gun by gravity, not pulled up by suction. For our purposes, the gravity-feed gun is the only way to go.

Figures 2 and 3 show different versions of gravity-feed guns, with the fluid container mounted up above the gun. A traditional high-pressure touch-up gun is shown in figure 2. There can be more overspray with these due to the pressure. A more modern high-volume low-pressure (HVLP) gun is shown in figure 3. Either of these two will give excellent results. The HVLP gun may cost a little more, but gives less trouble with overspray (glaze droplets that miss the pot, and land somewhere else).

1. Suction-feed spray gun, with container located beneath the spray gun. Not a good choice for a potter.

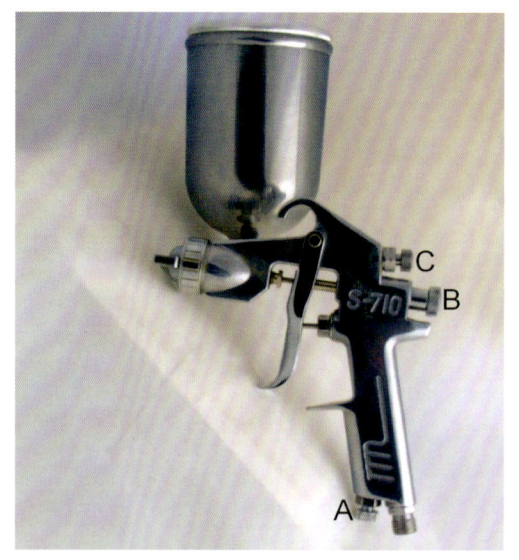

2. This high-pressure "touch-up" gun is a gravity-feed gun, with the fluid container mounted above the gun.

An advantage of a gravity-feed spray gun is the ability to measure the amount of glaze to be applied. That's important. Believe me. If the pot you're working on requires 45 mL of glaze, you simply measure out that amount, tip it into the gravity-feed cup, and spray until it's gone. Second, you can wash out the gun and change colors without wasting glaze or messing about cleaning the big pot that comes with a suction-feed spray gun.

How it Works

No matter what kind of gun you have, in addition to the trigger, it's likely to have three control knobs (figure 2).

- Knob A controls a needle-valve in the compressed air pipe. If you turn this knob all the way clockwise, the needle valve completely shuts, so if you pull the trigger nothing happens. No air comes out. As you turn the knob counterclockwise it opens the needle valve to let more air through. Most of the time, you open this just enough to get a spray of fine droplets of glaze without a great blast of excess air, which can create a mist of unwanted overspray.
- Knob B covers the end of a long needle valve, which controls the amount of fluid that escapes when you pull the trigger. If you unscrew knob B all the way (counterclockwise) you will find a spring underneath it, and the end of the fluid control needle will be revealed. Pull the long needle out. It has a pointed end that goes all the way through the gun, right up to the small hole where the spray comes out. You may sometimes need to pull this needle out when washing the gun, so you can squirt water down the little holes where it comes from. With the needle back in place, and the spring behind it, knob B can be screwed all the way in again. Now when you try to pull the trigger, you'll notice that it only moves a little way. The needle valve opens just a tiny bit, if at all, and not much fluid comes out. If you screw knob B out a bit more, the fluid needle can travel back further when you pull the trigger so more fluid comes out.
- Knob C controls yet another needle valve, this time feeding air to two tiny holes in the horns on each side of the spray nozzle (figure 4). Look closely at the spray nozzle end of the gun and you'll see it has three little holes. In the middle one, you may see the point of the fluid needle just sticking out a bit. This is where the fluid comes out. The two other little holes, in the horns of the

Basic Techniques and Tools

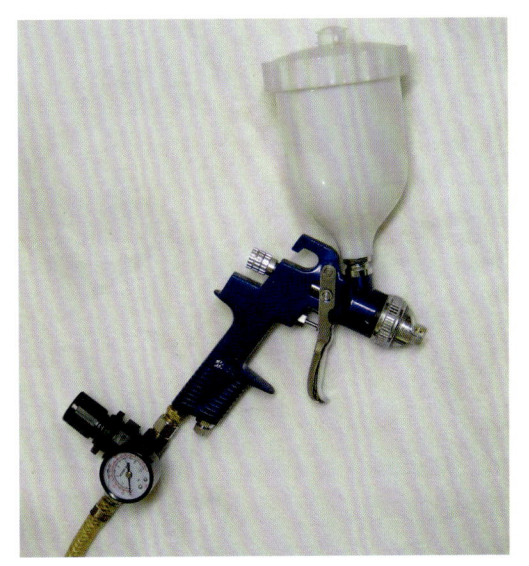

3. HVLP gravity-feed spray gun with the container on top. Lower pressure can reduce the amount of overspray.

4. Holes in each of the two horns on either side of the spray nozzle produce two fine jets of air that mix with the fluid sprayed from the center hole.

nozzle, are for air only. The horns produce two fine jets of air into the mist of emerging droplets to spread the pattern out into a fan shape instead of a narrow circular spray. The further you open knob C, the more air comes out of the horns and the more fan-shaped the spray pattern becomes.

- To try out a gun, put some water in the container and try adjusting the knobs. This is not a "set-and-forget" exercise. You'll find there are times when you want more or less fluid (knob B); a wider fan spray to cover a platter, a narrow one to put a fine accent band on a rim (knob C); or more or less air to suit the thickness of the glaze or the size of the droplets you desire (knob A). You'll be twiddling these knobs repeatedly as you change from pot to pot or from glaze to glaze.

You can also rotate the end of the nozzle, the part carrying the horns, so the fan-shaped spray comes out left-and-right (this is when the horns are at top and bottom), or to get a fan shape vertically up-and-down (when the horns are at left and right).

Compressed Air

You'll need an air compressor to use with the spray gun, but it need not be too large. A small machine with a modest storage tank is okay for a few seconds of spraying at a time. A larger compressor is needed for continuous spraying. Check your local home improvement store.

Checking the Spray Pattern

You'll need to check the spray pattern every time you adjust the knobs. Keep a rectangular piece of fiberboard inside your spray booth where you can give a quick spray and see what pattern it leaves.

Most of the time, you'll want a gentle spray of finely divided droplets carried by just enough air to give a smooth even coat. If the air control knob is open too far, you'll get a blast of excess air that makes the droplets smaller, but also carries many of them beyond the pot as overspray. At the other extreme, too little air results in a coarsely-divided spatter of slow-moving larger droplets, which may be exactly what you want for some effects.

Spraying Distance

Spraying glaze on a pot is not the same as spraying paint. You'll have to experiment for yourself, but here are some guidelines.

To spray a flat tile or a platter, holding the spray gun a distance of 6–8 inches away from the surface would be okay, with the spray pattern adjusted to a suitable width, say 3 inches or a bit more. In general, for a larger pot, increase the distance, use a wider spray pattern, more air, and more fluid.

- For a smaller, 6-inch wide pot, use less air, less glaze, and spray from a shorter distance.
- To add a highlight of a different glaze around the rim of a pot, close-up, throttle the gun back to a minimum amount of glaze in a narrow spray pattern, and hold it about 2 inches from the rim, perhaps even less, as you rotate the pot.
- When spraying a pot, slowly spin the turntable supporting the pot first, then pull the trigger to start glazing. If you want a thick, dense coat of glaze making a narrow band around a rim, but feathering out rapidly on either side, hold the gun much closer to the pot. No set distance suits all operations.

Cleaning the Spray Gun

To change from one glaze to another, you'll need to wash out the gun with a plastic trigger-spray bottle, the kind that can be adjusted to make a narrow stream or a wide spray.

If there's any glaze left in the cup, tip it back into the glaze container. Point the gun into the container and pull the trigger long enough to release last few drops of glaze. Give the glaze cup a quick squirt with the spray bottle, and spray the tiny amount of washing water back into the glaze container too. That gets rid of nearly all of the first glaze, without wasting any. Next, spray in more water, but spray it out of the gun down into the sink this time. Open the air control (see figure 2, knob A) a bit when you do this, to give it a good vigorous flush. Sometimes there's a residue of sediment partly filling the small pipe where the gravity-feed cup screws onto the gun. Unscrew the cup and look. A quick squirt with the spray bottle will clean out this pipe too.

When it seems that glaze doesn't come out as fast as it should, and repeated pulling of the trigger clears the blockage only for a while, it's time for more dismantling. There should be a wrench supplied with the spray gun just for this purpose. Unscrew the knurled ring that holds the horned spray nozzle and give it a quick squirt of water to clean it up. The trouble is further down, inside the pointed nozzle, where the end of the fluid control needle sticks out. You'll find the special wrench has a central hole with a square bit cut out that fits over the squared end of the nozzle. The nozzle may be tight, but it does unscrew. Wash or scrape out any residue. This cleaning takes two minutes.

Preparing and Storing Glazes

We normally sieve all our glazes with a 100-mesh sieve. An 80- mesh sieve also works to remove any particles that could clog the spray gun.

For glazes intended to be applied by spraying, two-liter plastic bottles are just the thing for storage. You can shake the bottle vigorously to mix it all up, and pour out as much as you need. And it's easy to transfer any leftover glaze back into the same container, straight from the gun, with just a little rinse out from a trigger-spray bottle. Even if the glaze is one you store in bigger quantities, keep a liter or two set aside in a bottle, to save all that stirring and dipping and washing out.

Glaze Thickness

If you're spraying the glaze on, how do you know when you've applied enough? If the glaze is brown, do you stop when the pot looks brown all over? It's easy to stop too soon, and get a glaze coat that is too thin and starved.

For best results, it pays to measure the density or specific gravity of the glaze when you mix it. What you're really measuring is how heavy the glaze is compared with pure water. For measuring the specific gravity of the glaze, use a hydrometer. Try this link to find instructions on making a hydrometer from a plastic drinking straw http://members.optusnet.com.au/rogergraham/floating_straw_hydrometer.pdf.

Every bucket of glaze in our workshop has the name of the glaze and the specific gravity clearly marked on the label, (usually 1.35 or 1.4). Glazes get thicker with time, by evaporation, so from time to time stir up the bucket, float the hydrometer, and add water if necessary. What matters is not so much what the specific gravity is, but that it stays the same every time you use it so you get consistent results.

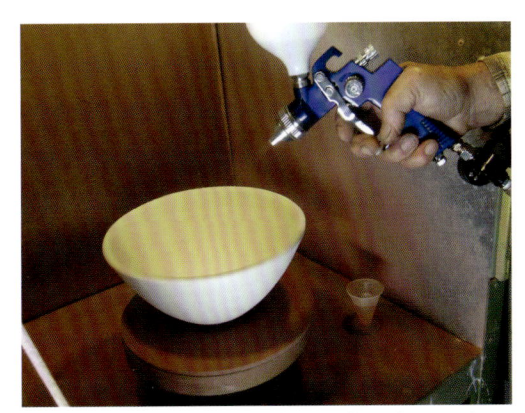

Basic Techniques and Tools

5. Spraying bowl interior: use less air, less glaze, and spray from a shorter distance.

6. When spraying the outside of a bowl, work with the form supported upside down.

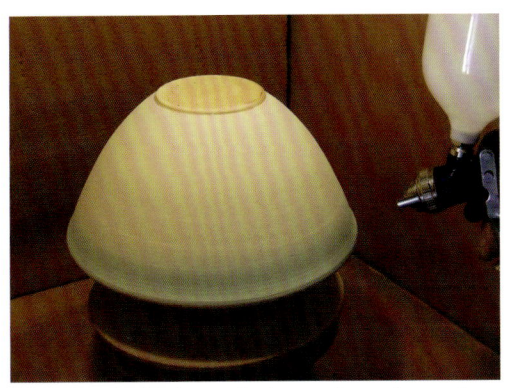

7. To add a highlight, work close to the surface and use a narrow spray pattern.

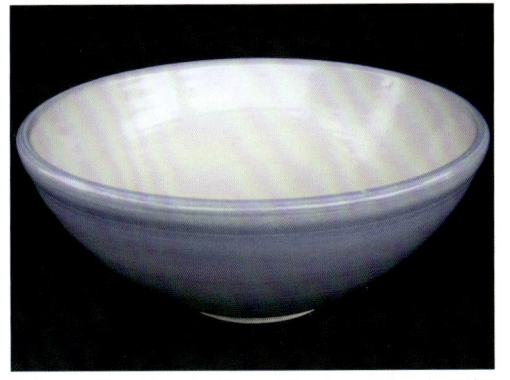

8. Spray-glazed bowl with a white glaze sprayed on the inside and a blue glaze sprayed on the outside.

Spraying Your Work

You'll need some kind of turntable or banding wheel to support the pot while you spray it. The idea is to slowly rotate the pot as you spray, and to access all sides. As you work, you need to be able to start and stop the wheel spinning, turn it slowly or not at all, by one hand alone. It's better to set this up in a spray booth but if you're just getting started at this, do your spraying outside. In either case, wear the appropriate NIOSH-rated and -approved respirator when spraying glazes.

Glazing different forms requires different strategies. The examples here cover glazing a bowl and a platter, but can be adapted for other forms.

Glazing a Mixing Bowl

This bowl will have a white glaze inside, pale talc blue outside, then a touch of a darker blue on the rim (see figure 8). Start with the inside. Evenly spray the inside to the desired thickness while rotating the bowl on the turntable (figure 5). Notice the distance between spray gun and pot. The emerging fan of spray is about 3 inches wide when it reaches the pot. To spray the outside of a cylinder-shaped pot, it's easy to get a uniform coat of glaze all the way down the wall, so the bottom gets as much glaze as the top. But when the pot tapers outward from a narrow base to a wider shoulder, things get more complex. One rotation of the turntable while spraying the wide shoulder gives a thinner coating of glaze to the shoulder than one rotation at the same speed while spraying the narrow base. This becomes a matter of judgment, so you spray a bit longer where the pot is a bit fatter. A common mistake is to spray too little glaze right down at the bottom, next to the

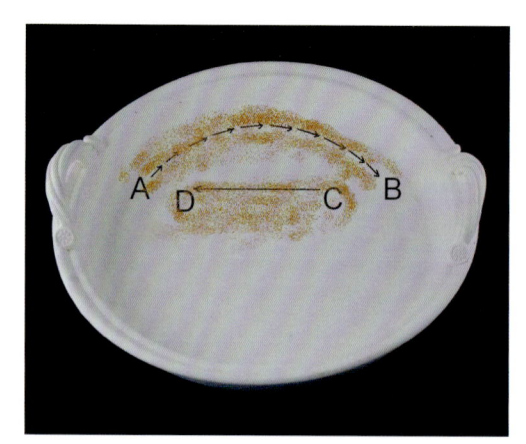

9. Diagram showing how to spray glaze onto a platter. Starting at A, move in an arc across the platter to point B, then from C to D.

foot of the pot, so you get a starved area down low. This is especially so if the pot curves away underneath, so the gun can't spray directly onto the pot from below. Spray the pot upside down, supported on a tall pedestal (figure 6).

Next, apply a narrow band of glaze on the rim, with just a little overspray thinning out rapidly on either side. You can do this while the bowl is still upside down to avoid getting the darker glaze inside the bowl (figure 7), or you can spray from above, but be careful. Hold the gun close to the rim and adjust the controls to give just a narrow spray, not much fluid, not much air. The darker blue glaze relies for color on 2% cobalt carbonate, and it's just faintly pink at first. To make it visible while spraying, add a few drops of cyan printer ink to the mix.

Spraying a Large Platter

To spray a large platter, start with the underside. Wax the base, and select a bat of suitable size to cover the waxed area. Shake up the glaze bottle, and transfer glaze into the cup on the gun. Figure 9 gives a good example of how to approach spraying glaze onto a platter. With the platter face down on the turntable, spray it evenly all around the rim. Clean up any overspray that crept under the bat. Turn the platter right-side-up, measure out the glaze once more, and do it all again. If you've not done this before, beware of a beginner's mistake here. You have this platter carefully centered on the turntable, and as it rotates you hold the gun a suitable distance from the plate as it spins around. If you gradually move the gun from the outside of the plate toward the center, the middle of the plate will acquire a thicker pool of glaze than the rest. Five seconds of spray on the rotating outer part of the plate gives a medium coat. The same time spent nearer the center gives a much thicker coat. This is where you'll have to use some judgment. Keep the turntable still. Apply a slow sweeping band of spray from A to B as shown in the diagram. Then make a quicker, lighter return stroke straight across the middle from C to D. Now rotate the turntable about a quarter of a turn and repeat. Continue this process all the way around. It still depends on your judgment to try and get a uniform coat, but it's easier to avoid that puddle-in-the-middle defect. When the measured amount of glaze is all gone, give the cup a quick squirt of water from a spray bottle to rinse it out. Spray this rinse water onto the platter, too.

Handles and Knobs

Before spraying the main body of the pot, dip a floppy brush with long soft bristles into the required glaze, and flood it smoothly into the difficult places. Feather the brushed glaze out at the edges so it blends in smoothly when you spray the rest. For those little crevices where a lug meets the body, flood in some glaze the same way as it would go if you dipped the pot instead of spraying.

A Final Word

If you want to glaze a big platter by dipping, then you'll need at least a couple of gallons of glaze. But to glaze it by spraying, you'll need maybe a cup at most. On this count alone, you can afford to experiment with a dozen glazes mixed in half gallon batches. And if you make notes as you go, you'll be able to repeat your successes with confidence so long as you have a record of how much glaze was applied to a given area.

Basic Techniques and Tools
SPRAYING GLAZES

by Kathy Chamberlin

Spraying glaze onto your ware, instead of dipping it or applying it by brush, can be an exciting way to vary your aesthetic results. By overlapping strokes and planning your coverage, you can achieve aesthetically interesting visual and textural results. Your success in spraying glazes depends as much on your preparation, your organization and your thoroughness as on your technique itself. Here's how to get the best results.

Setting Up the Spray Booth

To get set up, you'll need a spray booth; a spray gun; a banding wheel turntable; protective clothing, mask and eyewear; a five-gallon bucket and, of course, glazes. For me, an old fiberglass shower stall works great as a spray booth. It allows quick access to water, making cleanup easy. Placed upside down in the stall, the bucket comes in handy to elevate your work area. And it rinses easily when you're done and ready for clean-up.

Be sure to protect yourself from inhaling dangerous vapors or splashing glazes in your eyes. In an open booth, there can be a lot of glaze overspray, so I use a full face and head mask to prevent inhalation and glasses to shield my eyes from splatters or splashes. I always keep a pair of rubber gloves nearby.

Finally, you'll need a high-volume, low-pressure (HVLP) spray gun and a banding wheel or turntable for application of the glaze. Always strain and re-sieve each glaze before use to be sure it's uniform.

To prepare flat surface pieces, use a plate stand or simply hold it upright with your hand or lay it flat on top of the upside-down plastic bucket, and start spraying. To apply glazes to round pieces, you'll need the banding wheel or turntable. Place the banding wheel on top of the bucket and apply the glaze as you slowly turn the pot. Hand turning the banding wheel helps ensure complete glaze coverage and allows you to target specific spots.

Venting a Spray Booth

Provide proper and adequate ventilation to promote a safe work environment. Remove harmful emissions and materials when spraying glazes inside a room.

A typical and highly efficient venting system is a whole house ventilation fan set up to exhaust dust in the air. This type of fan needs a supply of fresh air to work properly. A low-tech venting system could be a bathroom or an over-the-stove fan to circulate air within the booth. The best system should not only be able to introduce fresh air, but also filter out the glaze oversprays. Always use a proper respirator when spraying glazes.

Decorating Before Spraying

If you like patterns to show through your glaze, you can decorate your work before glazing. I like to do detail line work with slips on leather-hard ware. You may need to experiment to be sure your lines don't run, and to see which glazes let the designs show through.

I use a lot of slips and underglazes when the ware is leather-hard, and glazes and oxide combinations after the bisque firing. If you plan to use color oxides over the glaze, it's handy to make a sketch of the designs to refer to when you lay out the color. When using oxide combinations, I tend to stay in the iron family, but also use a lot of copper and rutile together.

Also, mastering the pressure and release of brushstrokes, for example, leads to one of my favorite symbols, the bamboo leaf. Plastic squeeze bottles—with or without a metal tip—can be used for trailing slip.

Spraying

There are two keys to successful spraying: organization and endurance. The first step is getting organized, and for me that means having enough glaze ready to go so I don't have to stop midway through the application to refill a spray canister. I usually use two spray guns and up to six detachable canisters.

If I plan to use abstract shapes on flat pieces or to mask the inside or outside of baskets so I can glaze them with different colors, I cut these beforehand. The spray gun applies a lot of air pressure, so it may be necessary to tape or hold down the masking material.

The other key is endurance. Once I start, I like to spray all the ware I designate for a particular color before loading a clean canister and moving on to another color. I spray the glaze medium to thick. Since I like to layer a lot of glazes, and seldom pour glazes on clay, each piece has at least two spray applications.

Vertical surfaces like those in baskets also pose a challenge, since many glazes may flow quite differently. If it's hard to reach the bottom of a basket or other vessel, balance it on a small container like a yogurt cup and spray up under for good coverage.

When spraying several coats or layers of one glaze, allow each coat to dry before applying the next. I also use masks extensively to create a lot of abstract shapes and stenciling. When spraying baskets, cut outs from plastic plates can mask the inside or outside, so I can use different glazes that

A fiberglass shower stall serves as a spray booth for applying glazes. You'll also need a high-volume, low-pressure spray gun, a banding wheel/turntable, a face mask or respirator, rubber gloves and glazes.

Basic Techniques and Tools

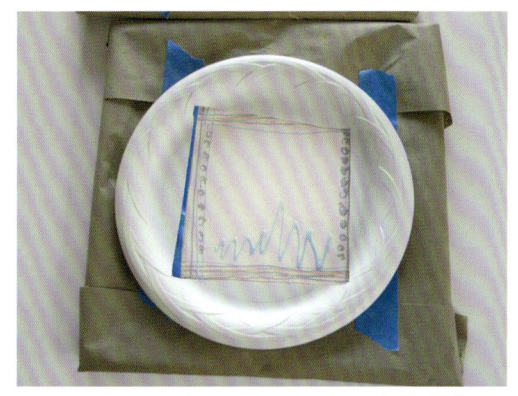

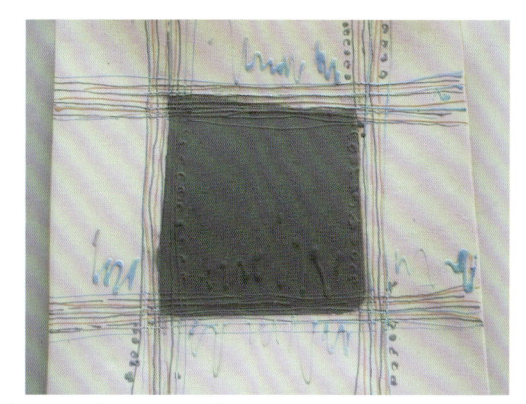

Use cut-outs to get interesting shapes and mask all areas where you do not want glaze. Here a square-cut out in a round, plastic dinner plate is used to produce a square of glaze.

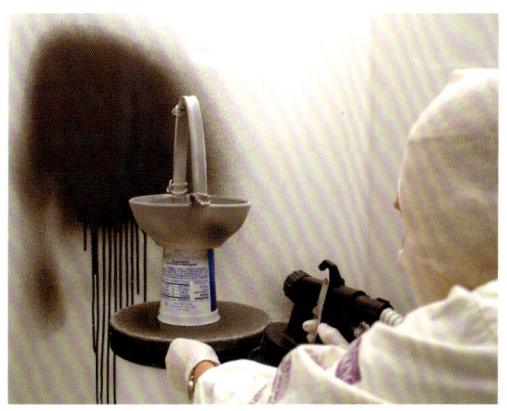

When spraying a basket, elevate it on a small container so you can spray up from below to ensure good bottom coverage.

Other decorative highlights designed to show through the glaze can enhance your piece.

may not interact well if overlapped. This method of using cut-outs to create sharp, clean lines and different overlapping glazes produces deep and beautiful flashing effects.

Glaze Information

I use three different shinos; yellow crystals; white, blue and black barium matts (applied with brushes); and green ash glazes (the best for transparency). I also use three different copper reds, but they are very temperamental. I usually put my green ash glaze under or over the copper red, or use a celadon. The oxides are mostly used in combinations: 1 part iron, 1 part rutile (half-and-half) and some cobalt. Dry wood ash is sprinkled on as surface decoration. I fire my work to cone 10–11 in a reduction atmosphere using a gas fired kiln. The techniques I use can be used with other types of glazes in different temperature ranges.

Clean Up

If you want to prevent problems with residual glaze, dust or glaze build-up on the spray gun, it pays to be obsessive about the cleaning of the spray booth and tools. I rinse out the shower; clean the spray guns with water and rinse each canister; then fill a canister with water and spray out the nozzle until it's rinsed clean.

With an improvised spray booth, a little preparation and a carefully thought-out plan, it's easy to produce interesting new looks on your finished ware with sprayed glazes.

Basic Techniques and Tools
RESISTS REVIEW

by Deanna Ranlett

There are many types of resists available that are designed to work on both greenware and bisque ware, including wax and latex. there are also many options involving re-purposing products and materials such as beeswax, stickers, tape, paper, acrylic medium, crayons, lipstick, Vaseline, and more!

The first thing to keep in mind when using any type of resist is whether or not it can be fired. Wax can be fired off in your kiln, while latex, paper, tape, etc., should be removed before firing because as they burn, they can carry and deposit glaze onto kiln shelves or other pots. Kilns must be well ventilated when firing any type of resist.

Commercial wax resists are produced by a variety of manufacturers and are available from your local supply shop. For our experiments, we used Forbes wax resist. It takes colorant easily, can be thinned down to layer between glazes, pipes easily with a needle-tipped bottle, and brushes well.

Also common are peel-off latex-based resists. These resists are allowed to dry and then are peeled off of the pot. If your surfaces have many tiny details and you feel like you won't find them after glazing, use regular wax resist.

Line resists, such as Artistic Line Resist (ALR), perform like a cross between a wax resist and a de-

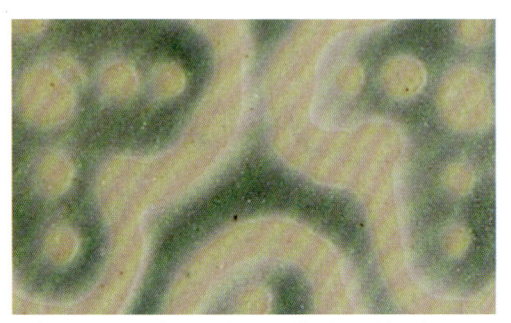

Forbes wax piped on with a needle-tipped bottle.

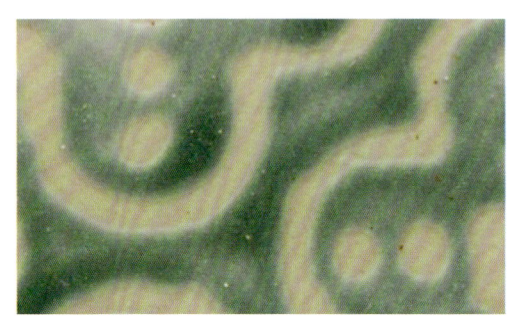

Mayco latex resist piped on with needle tip bottle.

ALR piped with needle-tipped bottle—spreads out a lot, fires to a brown color.

Wax resist colored with cobalt, shown reacting with a tin glaze and creating the purple, mottled effect.

cal medium. These resists are oil based and can be used in a variety of ways. You must use these products in a well-ventilated workspace, wear a respirator fitted with a vapor cartridge, and use a fan to divert fumes away from your workspace.

Melted wax can also be used. Many studios used to keep pans of paraffin wax melting at all times, but not only are the fumes hazardous—especially when wax heats above a certain temperature—but it can also be a dangerous fire hazard. I advise against this type of resist unless heated in small amounts and closely watched.

Megan Daloz, a resident artist at MudFire Clayworks, and I experimented with a variety of resist products. I only use wax resist when I want to create a crisp line when dipping glazes or to create layers of decoration between glazes. Megan, however, does a lot of intense surface decoration involving line work, sgraffito, and piping so we approached the resist exploration with her decorating style in mind.

Wax Emulsion Resists

Sources: Forbes (water based), Mobil (oil based), Laguna Mobilicer-A, Wax-On, Amaco Wax Resist, Mayco Wax Resist, Continental Clay Wax Resist, Aftosa black wax resist, Duncan Wax Resist

Pros: Wax was easy to brush, dip, pour, spray, pipe (had to use tiny tips on a squeeze bottle to avoid too much wax running), easy to wipe off the pot, resisted glazes beautifully, and is easy to spot.

We added food coloring to our wax resist to create a more noticeable mark on all clay bodies. Ceramic colorants (oxides and stains) can also be added to the wax to create interesting surface effects after the firing.

To experiment with this type of mark making, try the following recipes:

- Mix 1 teaspoon iron oxide with 1 teaspoon Gerstley borate and a touch of water to blend. Then add 6 to 8 tablespoons of wax resist and thin as necessary to make a pretty brown wax.
- Mix 1 teaspoon stain (I used black Mason stain) with 1 teaspoon Gerstley borate and a

Screenprinted ALR with red satin glaze, fires metallic at cone 6.

Megan Daloz uses underglaze, sgraffito, and various resists on her surfaces.

touch of water to blend, then add 6 to 8 tablespoons of wax resist and thin as necessary to make a beautiful black wax.
- Mix ½ teaspoon cobalt carbonate with 1 teaspoon Gerstley borate and a small amount of water to blend. Then add 6 to 8 tablespoons of wax resist and thin as necessary for a blue wax.
- Blends of oxides or stains can make some great colors: rutile and iron produce an orange surface similar to a soda firing.

Cons: When you make a mistake, the wax must be fired off in order to remove it, although some wax emulsions can occasionally peel off between glaze layers. Wax emulsions handle differently when doing tasks like screenprinting, slip trailing, or sandwiching (layering wax between glazes to allow patterns to be formed with overlapped glazes). It's important to find a wax you like to work with and one that works for you.

Latex Resist

Sources: Amaco Rubber Latex, Ceramic Shop Wax Off, Liquid Frisket, Aftosa Liquid Latex

Pros: Easy to brush (depending on the brand), and easy to peel off. You can easily apply latex over bisque and peel off to glaze that area or leave it alone. This makes glazing in the resisted area possible, where with other resist methods, you might need to fire first. With latex, you can immediately start glazing with your next color.

Cons: Sometimes thick glazes will cover the latex, making it hard to find and peel off. Firing latex can result in glazes flaking during the firing. Flakes can ruin shelves or other pots. Piping can be a challenge because latex can form bubbles. Note: People with latex allergies should not use this product.

Artistic Line Resist

Pros: Brushes and screens well, and pipes very well. Very versatile and can be fired at a variety of temperatures. Useful for cuerda seca style work. Similar to the oil-based decal mediums and makes a great decal when brushed or screened onto decal paper.

Cons: Doesn't resist brushed, sprayed, or dipped glazes well. Surface is wipe-able but not as much as a traditional wax resist. Stains the skin, has a strong odor, and must be used with a respirator fitted with a vapor filter, and preferably used outside or with a fan. When piping glazes, spreading occurred when we fired to cone 6. This resist is colored so you can't use it if you want your resisted area to be the color of your clay—line work will be a metallic brown at cone 6, black at cone 04.

Clean Up

In general, clean up is time consuming with all of these products. Take care of your brushes, cleaning them as quickly as possible after resist use. Some people swear by dipping the brush in Murphy's Oil Soap before using waxes and cleaning brushes with Shout or mineral spirits afterward. Use a separate set of brushes when using any type of resist. Clean your bottles, trays, and work area as soon as you finish—dried wax or latex in a bottle is no fun and any stray globs can easily find their way onto your pots.

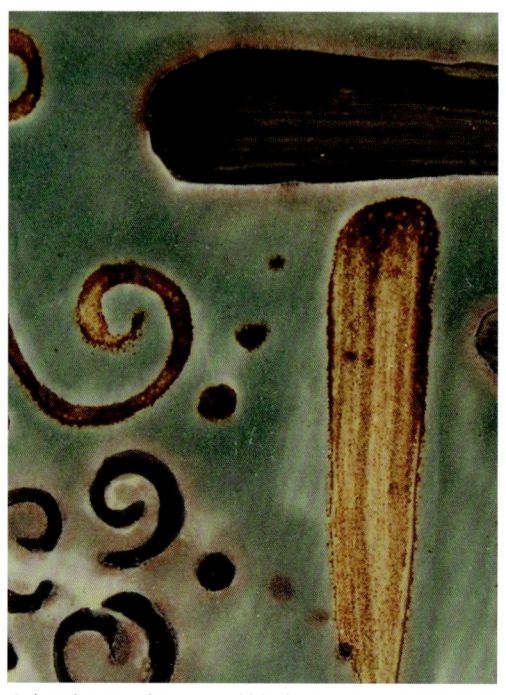

Colored waxes; brown and black. Experiment with both oxides and stains.

Basic Techniques and Tools
GLAZE DRIP PAN

by Jim Wylder

I routinely find myself needing an extra hand while pouring glaze over my pots. I solved the problem by using an automotive drain pan—typically used for changing oil in a car—that I attached to my pottery wheel like a throwing bat. Now I can center and secure various chucks to the interior of the drip pan to hold my pots and I can rotate the wheel as I pour glaze. I can also control how fast or slow I want to spin the pot depending on the decoration I choose for the surface. I also have the added benefit of collecting the glaze in an easy to clean container.

Cut a plastic cutting board into four chunks that are about 2 inches square each. Drill a ⅜-inch hole in one. Drill two overlapping ⅜-inch holes in the second one so that they create an oval. (Look at one of the newer plastic bats to see exactly how this looks.) Put the drilled chunks on your wheel-head bat pins, being careful to center the oval opening on the pin. Place the plain chunks near the outer edge, equidistant from the bat pins. Put silicone on the four chunks of cutting board and carefully lower the drain pan onto the wheel head. Slowly turn the wheel and center the pan. Put a bag of clay in the pan if you need weight to get a good seal. Let it set up overnight. You can also glue the drain pan to a plastic bat. If you decide to glue, be sure to seal the holes in the bat so the silicone won't glue the bat to the wheel head.

Materials and Tools

- Automotive drain pan (The one shown is 16¼ inches in diameter, holds 3½ gallons, and costs about $12 from an auto parts store.)
- Plastic ½-inch-thick cutting board
- Hand saw or table saw
- Drill and ⅜-inch drill bit
- Silicone caulk or construction adhesive

2

Graphic Patterns and Imagery
VINYL STENCILS

by Jay Jensen

The flat planes of the forms that I build create the perfect space to fill with pattern and design. Fired red earthenware has a beautiful color, which can also be a perfect backdrop for the glaze pattern.

My surface patterns are derived from sources such as the Modernist design movement, architecture, machines, and even sheet-metal design. My surfaces complement and contrast these references in congruent and sometimes incongruent ways. They are often inspired by textile and wallpaper designs from the early 20th century or even shower curtains and wrapping paper from the 21st century. I like the way they fill the open surfaces of my pottery and create visual interest while creating curiosity for the viewer.

I use Adobe Illustrator to design the patterns in silhouette. Again, a computer isn't necessary to make a resist pattern; you can make similar stencils with an X-Acto knife and clear contact paper.

After I've chosen a design, I send them to a sign shop to have them cut out of vinyl. I find that smaller shops welcome my business and are willing to work with my smaller orders. I get my vinyl cut in 24×24-inch sheets.

Applying the Surface Pattern

Start by adhering a layer of clear contact paper (the same stuff you buy for lining cabinets and drawers) to the vinyl patterns. The clear contact paper is necessary to keep the design intact. If you peel the backing off without it, it's impossible to put the sticker on the pot. Also if the design has parts that are "floating," the clear contact paper layer keeps the design together. Cut new templates (one each for the spout, funnel, and body) from the combined sheets of vinyl/contact paper using the templates originally used to make the ewer parts (figure 1).

The next step requires some practice and trial and error. Peel off the backing from the contact paper to reveal the sticky adhesive, then adhere it to the pot and use a hair dryer to smooth out any wrinkles and help it conform to the surface of the bisque (figure 2). Now carefully remove only the clear contact paper (figure 3). Next, decide whether you want to remove the negative or positive pieces of the design (figure 4). I try to mix it up on my work since my designs work well both ways. Now you're ready to glaze.

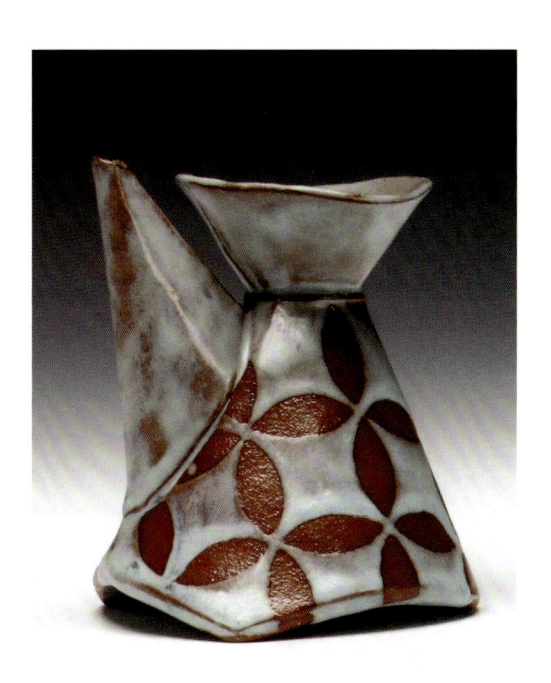

Ewer, handbuilt with red earthenware, decorated with cut-vinyl-resist pattern and glaze. *Photo courtesy of Schaller Gallery.*

Glazing Techniques

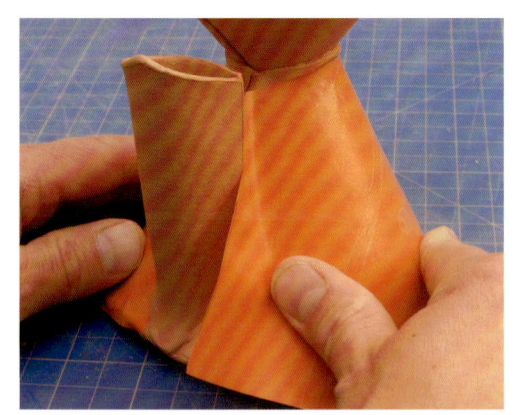

1. Apply contact paper/vinyl to the pot. Use a hair dryer to adhere the sheet.

2. Remove the contact paper from the form, leaving behind the vinyl stencil.

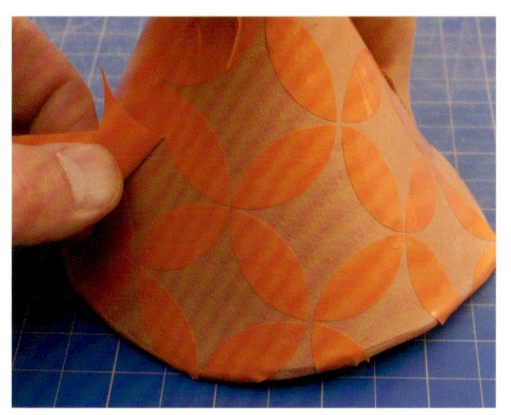

3. Remove either the negative or the positive shapes of the vinyl to reveal a pattern.

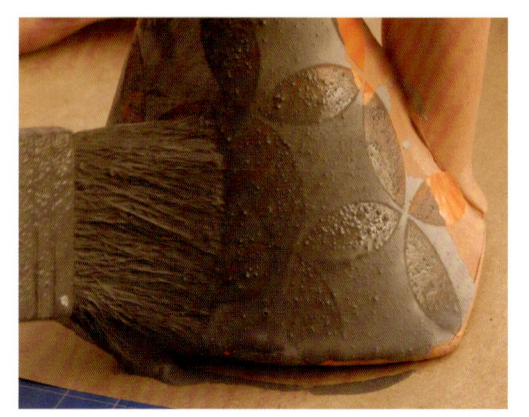

4. Apply the glaze over the vinyl stencil with a brush. Allow the glaze to dry.

Glazing can be done by dipping or brushing as well as adding slip, this depends on your own working preferences. I like use a brush for my low-fire glaze applications, this way I only need to mix very small quantities of glazes. Brushing glaze tends to work better for many low-fire glazes that have a little more forgiveness, while most high- and mid-fire glazes require a very even coating of glaze and dipping is preferred. Once the glaze is dry, use the tip of an X-Acto knife to gently lift off the remaining vinyl pieces (figure 5).

Since glazing in this manner exposes the bare clay, it's important that the clay have a nice fired color and surface on its own. I use a glaze recipe that contains a high-percentage of lithium and fumes onto the raw clay making the clay an even richer dark color.

5. Remove the remaining vinyl pieces using an X-Acto knife to peel up the edges, then fire the piece.

Graphic Patterns and Imagery
STAY-PUT STENCILS

by Roger Graham

This eucalyptus-branch platter was created by placing a metal stencil over a dark glaze then spraying a cream tin glaze on top.

The broad idea for stencils is to make use of two glazes, and apply one over the other. A stencil, lying snugly over the first coat of glaze, leaves an outline as the second coat of glaze is applied. For this to work well, the two glazes need to be of contrasting colors. They also need to be stiff and not too fluid when melted if you want the stencil outline to remain crisp and sharp. This process can be quite disappointing if either glaze is free-flowing and runny when hot.

Stencil Basics

When you set out to create a stencil, first decide on the shape and the size. Just one piece? Several pieces joined in some way? Or a loose group of completely separate pieces?

The stencil needs to be heavy enough to stay in place while you spray over it. Thin foil or sheet plastic tend to move under the force of the spray. You can weight down the edges of the stencil with small coins or fishing sinkers, but it's not easy with small detailed pieces. For stencils with fine detail, I use sheet lead. It's soft enough to cut with simple tools like scissors and sharp blades. I do not sand the edges of the stencils or do any other finishing process that creates lead dust, and I wear gloves when working with it. It's heavy enough to lie obediently in place while the second coat of glaze is sprayed over it. If the surface of the pot requires it, the soft malleable lead can be pressed down to make a snug fit against the piece. And finally, if you choose to assemble a number of small pieces, it's easy to do this using copper wire and solder.

If you do not want to work with lead, try a different material. Sheet metal (copper or tinplate) is harder to cut, though a jeweler's saw works well. It's not as flexible as lead, but a thin sheet flexes somewhat to be pressed snugly against the pot surface. These materials can be assembled using wire and solder for complex multipart stencils. Other materials that would work for making stencils that are washable and stay in place while spraying include heavier foam rubber or rubber floor tiles. These materials, and some sheet metals, can be found at hobby stores, home centers, and auto stores.

Types of Stencils

Here is an example of a one-piece stencil, a stylized Japanese bird (figure 1). The bird motif adds some interest to an otherwise plain and ordinary plate (see figure 2).

Glazing Techniques

1. Stencil of a stylized Japanese bird.

2. Platter with stylized Japanese bird motif, temmoku and copper red glaze.

3. Close-up of stencil showing small parts joined by wire bridges

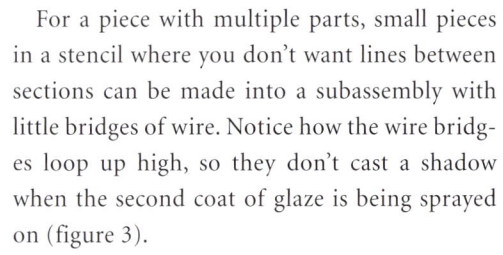

4. Eucalyptus-branch stencil with leaves and gum nuts joined by wires.

For a piece with multiple parts, small pieces in a stencil where you don't want lines between sections can be made into a subassembly with little bridges of wire. Notice how the wire bridges loop up high, so they don't cast a shadow when the second coat of glaze is being sprayed on (figure 3).

If your stencil has lots of little pieces, and you always plan to use the entire design in the same arrangement, it makes sense to connect them together. The leaves and gum nuts in figure 4 are all joined by stiff copper wire soldered to each one, so the whole thing can be lifted and repositioned in one simple move. The wire is placed flat next to the surface, so it leaves its own shadow to form the stems of the branch (figure 5). Note: If you use a different material, paste epoxy can be used to attach the parts and affix them to wires semi-permanently. Just make sure the end of the wire that touches the back of each piece either lays flat against it or that the end is bent into an L so that a short length lays flat against it. This will allow the epoxy to have more surface area to bond to.

More complex designs can be created using stencil elements composed on a plate in a different pattern each time they're used. The stencil for the *Fire Dancers* platter has at least 25 individual pieces (figure 6), and it's no small task positioning them all on the plate. The small pieces can be lifted off with tweezers after glazing, so you don't smudge the finished job. This type of stencil design is the reason that sheet lead is the material of choice. If the little flames were made of plastic, it would be very difficult to keep them in place.

Graphic Patterns and Imagery

5. Platter with stencil in place, ready for the second coat of glaze to be sprayed on.

6. A stencil with lots of pieces, the *Fire Dancers* motif.

7. Platter with stencil in place, second coat of glaze being dried with warm air before continuing to spray.

8. Platter with spraying completed, stencil removed, ready for touch-up if necessary.

Using Stencils

With the first coat of glaze in place, lower the stencil carefully into position so that it does not drag through the first layer of glaze (figure 5). Spray the second coat of glaze a little at a time, with the gun held not too close to the surface. The idea is to let the glaze mist down gently, evenly, and without having it blow in under the edges of the stencil.

If a pool of wet glaze builds up on the stencil, stop spraying and blow gently with warm air until it's dry before continuing (figure 7). When finished, use tweezers to lift off the stencil without dragging it around or leaving marks.

Look carefully at the resulting pattern (figure 8). Any little blobs of unwanted top glaze may be picked away with a pointed tool. Just don't dig too deeply into the bottom layer. Narrow tracks like leaf stalks may be improved by gently drawing something like a toothpick or a needle tool along the track. It's worth spending a few minutes here to get things right.

Fire Dancers platter, temmoku and copper-red glazes.

Graphic Patterns and Imagery
PROJECTING A PATTERN

by Shana Angela Salaff

I admit that I love playfulness as much as I love refinement! I strive to balance each piece with elegance and a sense of playful enjoyment. I do this by making formal choices in both categories.

Provided I join the separately thrown and hand-built pieces carefully, compress the seams well, avoid weakening them by adding too much water or stressing them with too much movement, then dry the completed piece slowly, I can avoid the anxiety of worrying about cracks showing up after the glaze firing.

Projecting the Pattern

Another way to banish anxiety is by projecting the pattern I decorate on the leather-hard surface using an old-school overhead projector—purchased for $20 at a thrift store. I have a freer line quality when I don't have to plan where to place the drawing. I find patterns in books or online, and discovered this particular pattern at a Haystack workshop. I use a scanner to save them to my computer, and then print them out onto acetate using my ink-jet printer so I can project the image. Very low-tech!

I spend time moving the acetate around on the projector until I get an interesting composition on the surface. I use an X-Acto knife to incise the pattern into the surface of the pot (figure 1). When the piece is bone dry, rubbing a green kitchen scrubby over the form removes the sharp edges created by the knife. After the bisque firing, I glaze the interior and the foot, then inlay a glaze saturated with chrome and copper that will fume and alter the color of any reactive glaze next to it into

I usually listen to audio books while I work. When completing the first *Mockingjay Vase*, I was listening to the *Hunger Games Trilogy*, Volume 3, which inspired me to name this work the "Mockingjay" series.

the incised lines (figure 2) and wipe away the excess with a clean, damp sponge (figure 3). I brush different glazes around the inlay areas to complete the pattern (figure 4).

I think that the formal name (for the theorists among us) for what I call playing is "flow." For me, flow happens when the critical part of my mind is able to slow down and allow a flexible, responsive energy to overtake precedence or habit. When the main technical issues have been resolved, my receptivity increases. I can take note of new ideas to improve technique or form as I discover them. Leaving a project brimming with fresh ideas gives me incentive to return to the studio for the next round.

Graphic Patterns and Imagery

1. Project your pattern onto the surface then use an X-Acto knife to incise the pattern into the surface.

2. Inlay a glaze saturated with chrome and copper into the incised lines. Use two coats if necessary.

3. Wipe away extra glaze using a sponge. Clean the sponge frequently to prevent colored streaks.

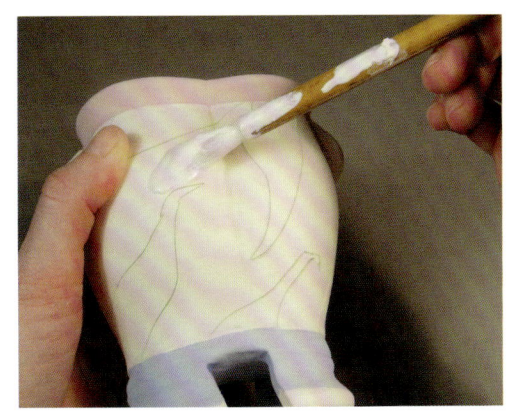

4. Brush different glazes into areas inside and outside of the leaves. Try to leave the incised lines showing.

Mockingjay Vase #2, Laguna B-mix 5 clay, various glazes, fired to cone 5.

35

Graphic Patterns and Imagery
POUNCING AND COLORING PATTERNS

by Susan Mussi

My work involves a type of surface decoration known as in-glaze or majolica decoration. Bisque fired pieces are covered with an opaque glaze base and then decorated with colors and they are fired together at 1796°F (980°C). I create realistic designs such as trees, figures, houses, etc., and these can be time consuming to draw. I rely on a traditional, low-tech method called *pouncing*, so that once these design elements are drawn, they can be reused multiple times, and put together to form different patterns on plates, pots, and tiles.

Pouncing essentially turns a drawing into a type of stencil. To pounce is literally to jump up and down. Pouncing as an art term refers to moving your hand up and down, pricking holes through the outlines of a design drawn on paper so that it can be used as a pattern. When finished, it's laid onto whatever surface is being decorated, and it's rubbed with a marking bag. This is a permeable bag filled with a colored powder that goes through the holes and marks the outlines of the design onto the base.

To pounce a design, you have to make a pin-pencil. Force a pin into one end of a pencil or rod of wood with pliers, then cut the head off. Take the pin out, turn it around and stick the blunt end into the hole you've made, forcing it in as much as possible, so it is firm and straight. Tip: For safety, when the tool is not being used, stick the point into a cork or rubber eraser.

Creating the Pattern

Draw the basic outlines of the design and the four sides of the tile to the size needed, and print it on transparent paper.

Lay a thin piece of cloth over a hard surface. Flip the tracing paper, so the backside is facing up, lay it on top of the cloth and punch holes through the outlines (figure 1). Don't punch holes in the

1. Using a pin tool, punch holes through the surface of the drawing.

2. Fill a marking bag with graphite and coat the surface of a tile with a base glaze.

Graphic Patterns and Imagery

3. Place the design and rub the marking bag over the pattern until powder transfers through the holes.

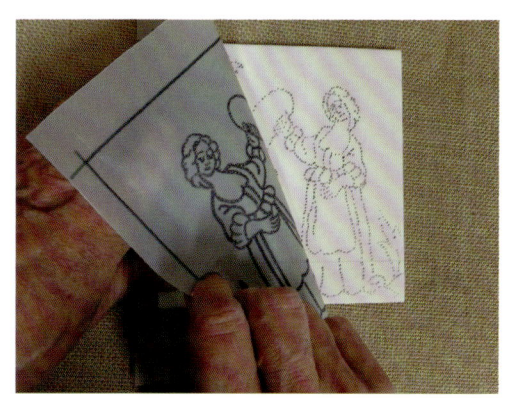

4. Lift up a corner to see if the powder is transferring correctly and clearly.

5. Using the powder lines as a guide, paint the border and outlines using overglaze.

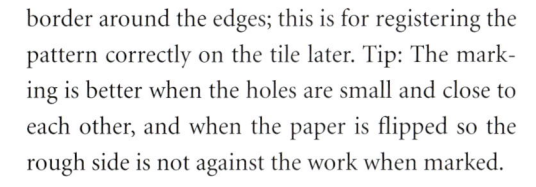

6. Fill in the interior of the design using majolica overglaze colors, then fire.

border around the edges; this is for registering the pattern correctly on the tile later. Tip: The marking is better when the holes are small and close to each other, and when the paper is flipped so the rough side is not against the work when marked.

Transferring the Design

First, you'll need to make a marking bag. Cut out a square from a piece of semi-open weave cotton cloth (a sheet works well), and place powdered graphite, charcoal, or talcum powder in the center. Lift up the corners, close them with a rubber band and you have your marking bag. Store it on a small plate as it makes everything dirty (figure 2).

Hold the pounced design against what you are decorating; here it's a bisqued tile covered with an opaque glaze base. To decorate, tap and rub over it with the marking bag, so the powder goes through the holes and marks the outlines of your pattern onto the raw, unfired glaze surface (figure 3). Lift up a corner to be sure it's well marked (figure 4).

Once the pattern is transferred, use the dotted lines as a guide to paint the outlines and to create a border around the edges if desired (figure 5). Both graphite and talcum powder burn away when fired. Paint the outlines first with a dark color then brush off residual graphite powder with a large, soft brush that's dry and clean. Then paint on overglaze colors (a ratio of one part colorant to three parts transparent glaze mixed with water and sieved). The densities of a color can vary, the movement of the paint brush strokes can be seen, and one color overlapping another forms a third color. The glaze firing fuses the colors and the base glaze to leave a beautiful, smooth, glossy surface (figure 6).

37

Graphic Patterns and Imagery
CREATING GEOMETRIC PATTERNS

by Anthony Merino with Pam Luke

Throughout my personal experience as an artist, I have found that more complex and difficult problems are most often solved by simple and obvious solutions. Several years ago, I needed to figure out how to paint patterns on pots. This created a dilemma for two reasons. First, patterns require grids and second, most pots are spherical. Mapping a grid on a round surface is difficult. To do it correctly, both the width and the height of the columns and rows need to expand proportionally with the diameter of the pot. The obvious solution would be to figure out how to calculate the expansion and measure out the grid. The drawback of this solution? Revisiting trigonometry and calculus. I didn't want to do that, so I had to learn to cheat. I figured out a way to put a grid on a round surface using a modicum of math ability and some very simple tools. This process requires paper, a 360° protractor, an X-Acto knife; water-based markers, and a drafting template.

Anthony Merino's raku-fired vase with tumbling block pattern.

Make a Template
Place the protractor on a sheet of paper. The heavier the stock of paper, the better. Drafting paper makes for a very good template. Using a pen, outline the circle on the piece of paper. Divide the circle into the number of segments you want on the pot. For this example, we'll create a pattern using six segments. Next, place a mark at each segment on the piece of paper. Finally, using the X-Acto knife, remove the circle from the center of the paper. The remainder of the sheet becomes the template with which you will lay out the columns for your pot.

Most 360° protractors are only 6 inches in diameter. If you need a larger template, mark the center of the circle, then draw a line using the center and each of the marks you placed on the outside of the circle. This line should extend past the desired circumference. Simply draw a larger circle using a compass.

Transfer the Template to the Form
Place this template over the neck and on to the shoulder of your bisque ware. Try to center the template as accurately as possible. You may want to put the piece on a banding wheel and make some light pencil lines to help center the template.

Graphic Patterns and Imagery

1. Place the pattern on the pot and use a water-based marker to transfer the dots to the pot.

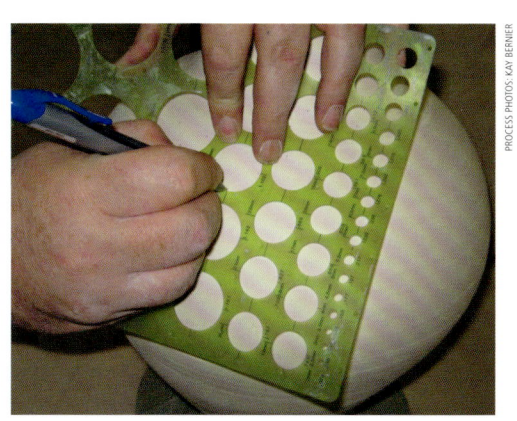

2. Create a second row of dots using the quadrant markers on the circular template.

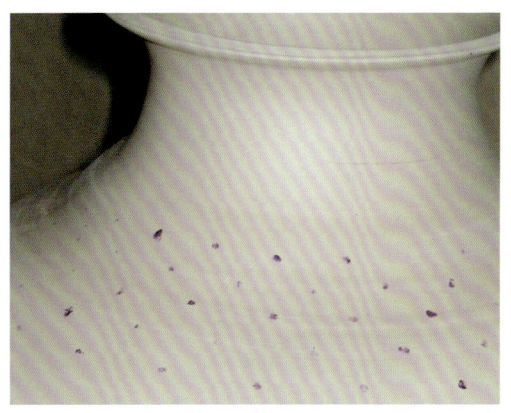

3. To continue the diamond pattern as the diameter of the pot increases, work with larger circles.

4. For a square pattern, either skip every other row, or place new dots between each existing dot in a row.

Next, using a water-based marker, place a mark on your pot that aligns with each of the marks from your template (figure 1). I have found that water-based markers work best for two reasons. First, they burn out when fired and second, they don't act as a resist when you begin to paint your pattern on the piece. After this step is complete, you'll have a circle of evenly spaced dots around the top of your piece.

Laying Out the Pattern's Grid

To lay out the grid, you'll need a drafting template, which is a flexible plastic sheet containing a collection of incrementally increasing circular holes. Each circle is segmented into quarters with marks (at 0°, 90°, 180°, and 270°). Take the drafting template and align one of the quarter section marks with one of the marks you placed on the pot. This will be considered 0°. Align the opposite quarter section mark horizontally with the next mark in the top row that you placed on the piece. This is considered 180°. Next, place two marker dots on the pot, one that aligns with the 90° segment mark on the template, and one that aligns with the 270° segment mark (see figure 2). Repeat this with every segment of your pot. When you finish marking, you will have created a second row of dots on your pot.

Repeat this process using the rows of dots you just placed on your pot as a reference to create a second row. As you do this, you'll notice that the dots in this row are spaced slightly further apart than the first row. In order to get an accurate spacing, you'll have to go to one of the larger circles in the drafting template to put down the next line of dots (figure 2).

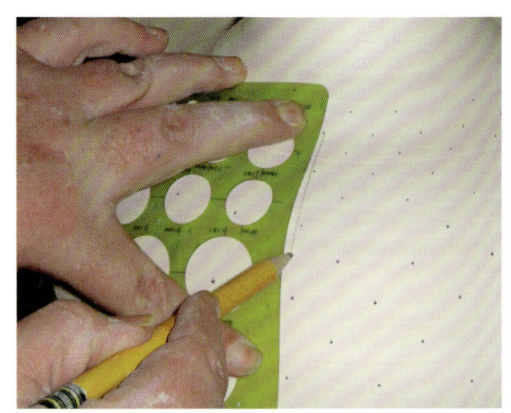

5. Mark a vertical line by connecting the dots using a pencil and the flexible drafting template.

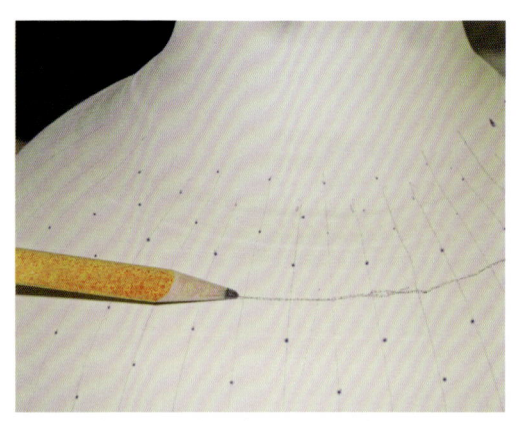

6. Create horizontal lines first by using the template to connect a few dots, then continuing freehand.

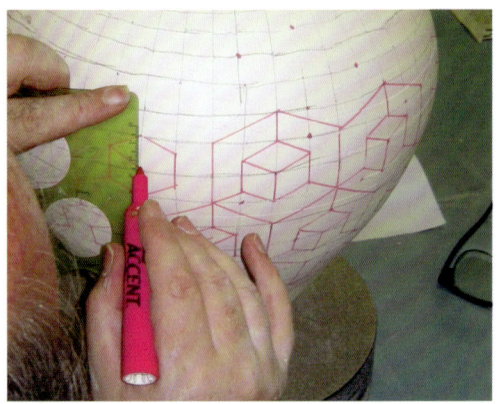

7. This tumbling block pattern uses an alternating grid to create boxes, so connect dots to begin your pattern.

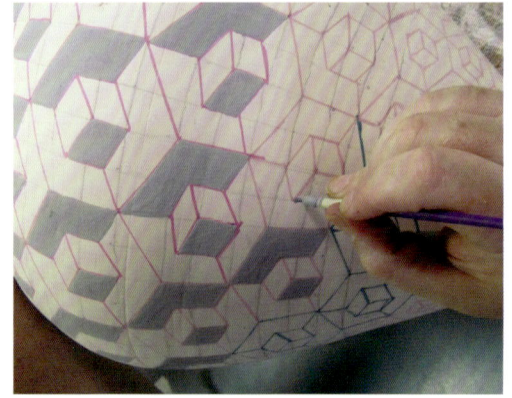

8. Using one glaze on at a time, fill in all segments of the pattern at one time for that color.

Repeat this process as you work up and down the pot. As the pot expands, you'll need to find a circle on the drafting template with a diameter that's as wide as the spacing of the dots on your pot. When you are done, you'll have a pot with an evenly laid out grid of diamonds (figure 3).

Changing from a Diamond to a Square Grid

The grid you completed in step three should appear to be comprised of diamond shapes. There are two ways to change this into a grid of squares. First, you can simply skip a row and column. Every other mark should align vertically. Using a slightly darker marker, put an additional dot after every other dot (figure 4). If you use this method to construct your grid, you do have to understand you will need to double the amount of segmentations for your pattern. So if your pattern requires two segments, you will need to section the vase by 4. Connect the marks you put on the piece with pencil lines to make the grid easier to see. To create the vertical lines, simply lay the edge of the drafting template against the pot and draw a vertical line that connects the dots (figure 5). Since the edge of the template is both flexible and straight, it's an excellent tool for drawing vertical lines on your pot. Next, draw the horizontal lines on your piece. First, using the edge of the template, line up two of the marks, create a pencil line connecting the two, then continue on to the next line (figure 6). You'll end up with a checkerboard-type grid. Make sure the dots for the shapes you want to create are clearly visible and stand out from the grid.

Graphic Patterns and Imagery

9. Raku-fired vase by a student at Anadolu University, Eskisehir, Turkey, made using the pattern grid technique with shapes created by modified intersecting circles.

Now that you have the grid laid out on the pot, drawing a pattern is relatively easy. As you go through the process of defining the pattern, start with lighter colors and move to darker colors the closer you get to the finished pattern you desire. Depending on your skill, you can choose to draw a complex pattern or one that is easy. Inspiration for many common patterns such as the tumbling block can be found in quilting designs, Islamic tile work, and even the 1980s-era computer game Q*bert. The tumbling block pattern can be created by alternating the grid on your pot. Place a dot on every other segment horizontally and every segment vertically. Using your marker, draw a line between these two marks. This will create a grid that allows you to create a box-like pattern (figures 7–8).

A fish-scale pattern is made by simply using your grid as a guide and drawing a line of circles around the piece. The circles should skip a row. Then on the row above and below—place a row of circles between the rows you created.

Another easy pattern is one that is similar to the sole of a Birkenstock sandal (sometimes called an apple core or an ax pattern), which is created by alternating the orientation of each quarter of your circle. The curve of the first quadrant (1° to 90°) and the third quadrant (181° to 270°) should alternate, curving out from the center. The curve between the second quadrant (91° to 189°) and the fourth quadrant (271° to 360°) should alternate, and should curve in toward the center of the circle. The resulting glaze pattern, after firing looks like this (figure 9).

Glazing Options

I developed this process for raku using a combination of commercial and metallic raku glazes because both are well suited to being applied using a brush. Most high-fire glazes don't look as good when painted onto pots as they do when glaze is applied through spraying or dipping techniques.

Several other options are available when it comes to glazing your pieces. One option is to brush on underglazes, then coat with a clear glaze. Removable masking materials like latex or masking tape can be used when painting your piece. These materials allow you to cover sections of a piece, dip or spray the glazes you want, and then go back in and uncover some areas while protecting others with wax or latex-resist and spray or dip the piece again in a contrasting glaze to coat the bare areas. If you want to use three or more different glazes, just repeat these steps. Another method you may want to consider is glazing the piece first. After the piece is glazed, you can paint a grid on it using food coloring, which burns out during the firing. After you establish a pattern, paint stains or oxides on top of the glaze.

The ultimate test for a technique is to try it in a workshop setting. I've demonstrated this system at workshops from Arkansas to Turkey. Once demonstrated, all students were able to easily create beautiful, proportional patterns on their pieces. This solution and a small amount of patience is all you need to create your own patterned pots.

Graphic Patterns and Imagery
LESS IS MORE

by Courtney Murphy

Combining clean lines and spare but playful decoration gives Courtney Murphy's work an inviting, slightly retro feel.

After all of those years working in white clay, I had a huge supply of underglazes. I didn't want the jars to go to waste, so I started testing all of my colors over the majolica to see what would happen. A surprising number of the underglaze colors looked great, those that didn't were very dry or bubbled. I put a big 'X' on those and boxed them up, so that I wouldn't accidentally use them. The colors I use are mainly Amaco Velvet underglazes and Duncan underglazes. Testing is required as certain colors will work fine, but a similar shade won't work. I often mix the colors that do work to create new shades.

Terra Sig

After switching to earthenware, I started brushing two to three thin layers of a terra sigillata on the bottom of bone-dry work to enhance the color of the clay and create a nicer feel on the bottom. Once the sig has lost its sheen, I burnish it by wrapping a plastic grocery bag tightly around my thumb and rubbing the coated area (figure 1).

Glazing and Decorating

After the work has been bisqued to cone 04–05, I begin glazing. I don't use wax, mainly because I'm pretty clumsy with it. Instead I scrape the excess glaze off with a rubber rib, then sponge the rest off, leaving about ¼ inch of the clay exposed on the bottom. To cut down on drip marks, once the glaze has dried a little, I use a soft drywall screen to sand out the larger drip marks. I always wear a dust mask and sand while holding the piece away from myself and over a bucket of water to minimize dust (figure 2).

Because the glazing and decorating process takes a while, glazing is done in small batches. I using three different colored versions of my base glaze: yellow, pale mint green, and white. I try to focus glazing with one color at a time, otherwise it gets confusing, as all of the glazes look the same in the bucket. This helps me to avoid touching up a piece with the wrong color.

Graphic Patterns and Imagery

1. Apply terra sigillata to the foot of a bowl then burnish with a plastic grocery bag.

2. Clean glaze off of the bottom with a sponge then use drywall screen to sand out glaze drips.

3. Using an 18-gauge slip trailer to draw lines on a bowl.

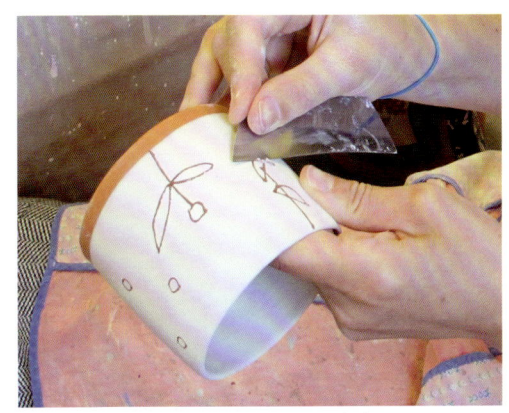

4. Scraping off a mistake with a metal rib.

When I first switched to majolica, I knew that I would miss the precision of the incised lines, but found that an 18-gauge slip-trailing bottle creates a very nice, fine line (figure 3). A 16-gauge bottle will form a thicker line. I use this less often, but it is useful for drawing dots on pieces. I fill the bottle with underglaze and add water if needed to get a smooth flow. Before drawing on a pot, test that it's flowing evenly on a piece of paper. Globs do happen occasionally, but they are easy to clean up if you let them dry then scrape them off of the surface using a metal rib (figure 4). After scraping, rub out that spot with a finger and redraw the line.

There is definitely a window of time when this process works best. I start drawing lines on top of the majolica about a half an hour after glazing. Line drawing comes fairly easily as long as the glaze doesn't get too dry and powdery. Once it has reached this stage, the slip trailer does not flow as easily. Lightly misting the glazed piece with water sometimes helps, but it's much better to decorate while the glaze still has some moisture in it.

When not in use, I plug the slip-trailing bottles with a sewing pin (the type with a little bead on the end). This works really well, and it's nice to have the pin available in case the tip gets clogged. It's important to remember to keep the pin in the tip when the bottles aren't in use, because they dry out easily.

The line drawings dry really quickly. Usually I'll draw on five to six pots, then start coloring in my drawings (figure 5). For the painting stage, I find it easier to pour my underglazes into a plastic ice tray, preferably one with a lot of compartments. The empty compartments are good for mixing underglaze colors together.

43

Glazing Techniques

5. Painting with underglaze over majolica.

Finished creamer and sugar with yellow majolica glaze.

Drawing Inspiration

My drawings aren't planned out beforehand; I tend to work more intuitively, looking at the space and seeing how I want to divide it up. I've spent the last two years trying to find the right balance between too little and too much decoration.

My drawings are mostly inspired by the idea of connection. I have moved a lot over the past several years and being in a residency situation involves a lot of people moving in and out of your life. Some of these connections have stayed very strong despite the distances. My drawings often occur in groupings of two to three similar elements, dotted lines sometimes connect these elements, creating lines of communication.

I'm also intrigued by the new connections that are formed when a pot leaves my studio to become a part of somebody else's life. I find this to be one of the most interesting aspects of being an object maker. Using pots made by friends who are far away really does help me to feel connected to them. It's a really nice part of being a potter.

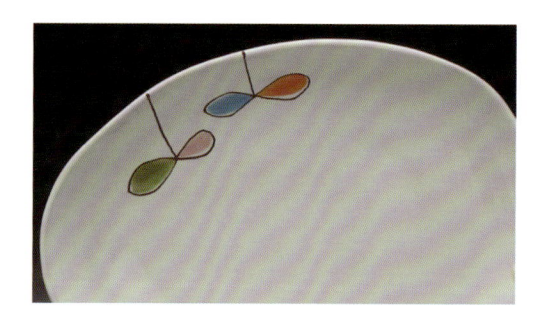

MEL'S FANTASTIC SIG

Redart	1 part
Distilled Water	2 parts
Add: Darvan 7	0.025%

(.025% of the clay weight, not of both the clay and water combined)

Blunge Darvan into water. Slowly add clay to water and blunge for about 3–5 minutes. Ball mill for 12–24 hours (no longer or shorter). Pour into clear container, let sit for 12–18 hours. Either siphon out middle layer, or just pour off the top 2 layers. The top layer of water should be minimal so its not usually worth siphoning.

Simmer gently on the stove, stirring constantly, until the mixture reduces itself to about 2/3 its original volume. If a skin forms on the surface while you're simmering it, just mix it back in. Save all chunks of clay.

When the sig cools, use a brush to re-integrate all the chunks and the liquid sig. There should be a slight sheen on the surface and the material should brush smoothly onto bone-dry pots.

I realize this is a more elaborate sig recipe than others you might have seen. I've tried simpler recipes, but had a lot of problems with flaking or weird textures. Finally, my friend Mel Griffin gave me this recipe and it's worked really well.

PB MATTE MAJOLICA
Cone 05–01

Dolomite	10 %
Ferro Frit 3124	65
EPK Kaolin	20
Silica	5
	100 %
Add: Zircopax	10%

Although this glaze was formulated to be a satin matte at cone 05, I have been firing it to cone 01. To tint the glaze, I add between 1–6 percent Mason stain.

Graphic Patterns and Imagery
SLIP AND SGRAFFITO

by Kristin Pavelka

Tidbits and more! Patterned plates may have different motifs, but the drawn shapes and layers of colorful satin glazes complement one another so well that they can be mixed and matched, just like your favorite appetizers.

I fell in love with red earthenware after viewing Iranian sgraffito wares of the 11th and 12th centuries. I enjoyed the casual application of glaze as it moved beyond its established etched boundaries or dripped down the sides of the outside wall. The pots displayed a depth and softness of surface that I was excited to utilize in my own work while putting a contemporary spin on these beautiful historical pots. My work blends ideas from these Iranian wares as well as sugary confections, mid-century and Scandinavian patterns, personal surroundings, and the styling of Martha Stewart.

Process

I slip my pots when they look dry but have a small bit of moisture in them. This allows for a relatively even coating of slip, yet it dries a bit slower giving me time to complete my sgraffito before the slip starts to chip when scratched. Because the slip dries quickly, I have to work fast to complete my design, so I plan the patterns ahead of time in a sketchbook or by drawing with a soft pencil on the unslipped plate itself.

Holding the plate vertically, I pour the white slip onto the middle of the plate using a large ladle, turning the piece clockwise until the entire face is covered (figure 1). Keep the plate vertical until the slip drips have firmed, then rest the plate on the tabletop and allow the slip to dry for a few minutes until you can touch it without a fingerprint remaining, but while it still feels cold and damp.

Lightly draw a grid on the piece using a soft pencil. Breaking up the space symmetrically on a circular form is a quick and easy way to understand the space. I sometimes draw my pattern on the piece to double check the placement of key elements, but usually I draw directly with my sgraffito tool using just the grid as an aid for placing the design.

My sgraffito tool had a previous life as a dentistry tool and is thicker and duller than a standard

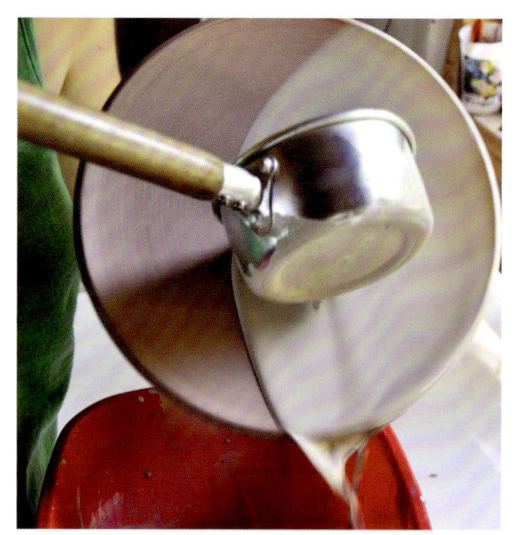

Glazing Techniques

1. Pour white slip onto the middle of the plate, turning the piece clockwise until the entire face is covered.

2. Scratch through the slip so that the tool just barely digs into the underlying clay.

3. Brush the surface once the design is complete to clean up the edges of the incised lines.

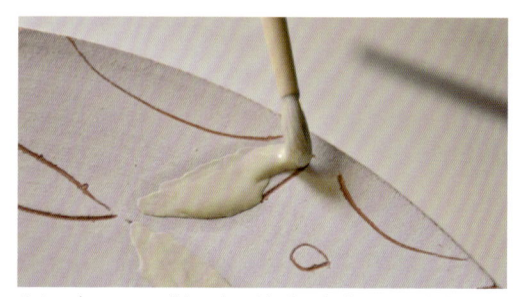

4. Load up a small brush with the darker-toned glaze and fill in the pod shapes on the bisque-fired plate.

needle tool. The line created is thicker than an X-Acto blade or needle tool and can give a similar line quality as a standard-sized pencil lead. Medium pressure is exerted with the tool tip so that it scratches through the white slip and just barely digs into the red underlying clay (figure 2). I brush a stiff yet soft-bristled brush across the surface of the plate once the design is carved to clean up the edges of the incised lines as well to rid the surface of the slip crumbs (figure 3). A Scotch Brite pad is lightly rubbed along the rim to help expose the red earthenware beneath. This final touch helps create a little more depth to the surface once it has gone through the glaze firing. Note: For all three of the above steps that create crumbles or fine powder, wear a mask and work over a bucket of water to minimize the amount of dust.

Glazing by Numbers

I bisque fire to cone 01, then, to prepare the piece for glazing, give it a good shower under running water to clean any leftover sgraffito dust from the surface. Leave the piece to dry overnight. The first glaze application is like a paint-by-number painting. Often using two tones of the same color, I'll load up a small brush with the darker tone and fill in the "pod" shapes. Little pressure is used when painting as the glaze should flow from the brush onto the bisque, eliminating brush strokes (figure 4). I fill the sgraffito lines with this first glaze, which helps eliminate pinholes in the glaze-fired impression. This first layer of glaze is left to dry several hours or even overnight.

The second, lighter tone of glaze is then poured on the plate in a similar fashion to the white slip—

Graphic Patterns and Imagery

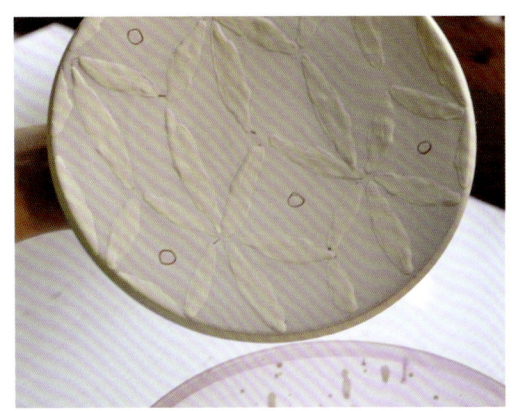

5. Once the glaze is dry, apply a lighter-toned satin glaze using the same technique as for pouring the slip.

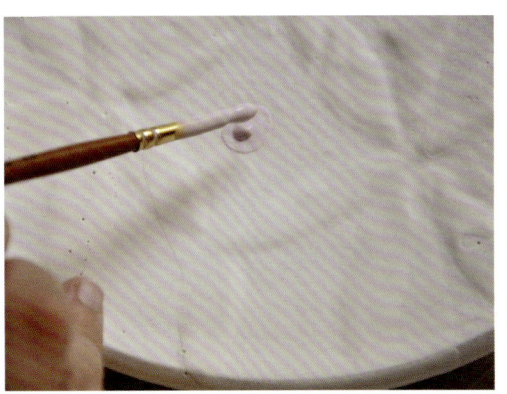

6. Apply the accent glazes, starting with the lighter glaze, and finishing with small dots of darker glaze.

rotating a vertically-held plate clockwise while pouring the glaze in the middle of the piece (figure 5). This second coat is left to dry.

The final glazes are now ready to be applied to the dots using a small soft brush or a fingertip. I can usually see a light indentation of the sgraffito dot through the poured glaze to use as a guide for dot placement. If I am unable to determine where to place my dot within the design, I sometimes guess and other times fire the piece and then apply the dots to the fired glaze and refire. The final dots are made up of a lighter-toned large dot with a smaller dark toned dot on top (figure 6).

The dry, glazed piece is fired to cone 04, held at that temperature for 15 minutes and then fired down to cone 010 before being turned off. This schedule helps to produce a nice satiny finish to the glaze surface.

PETE'S FORGIVING WHITE SLIP
Cone 04

Talc	40 %
Nepheline Syenite	10
OM4 Ball Clay	40
Silica	10
	100 %

Apply to leather-hard, bone dry, or bisqued clay.

SATIN BASE
Cone 04

Ferro Frit 3124	65.5 %
Nepheline Syenite	11.0
EPK Kaolin	5.5
Silica	18.0
	100.0 %
Add: Bentonite	2.0

I use Mason stains to color this glaze. For the plate shown (right), the dark yellow is 4% MS Vanadium Yellow 6440, the light yellow is 2.5% praseodymium yellow 6450. Light and dark pinks are 1% and 2% MS Crimson 6003.

WORTHINGTON CLEAR
Cone 04

Gerstley Borate	55 %
EPK Kaolin	30
Silica	15
	100 %

Use this base glaze along with colorants to create red and orange glazes. Used with 10% Degussa Orange stain for orange dots on the plates.

KAT RED
Cone 04

Wollastonite	13.7 %
Ferro Frit 3195	42.5
EPK Kaolin	23.5
Silica	10.7
	100.0 %
Add: Bentonite	2.0 %
Degussa Bright Red stain	12.0 %

Opaque, fat-looking satin glaze. Used to make the dots.

"FROSTING" MAIOLICA
Cone 04

Ferro Frit 3195	54.8 %
F4 Feldspar (Minspar 200)	14.3
Georgia Kaolin	4.5
EPK Kaolin	4.5
Nepheline Syenite	5.2
Zircopax	16.7
	100.0 %

This glaze has the look of marshmallow when layered on top other glazes.

47

Graphic Patterns and Imagery
PENNSYLVANIA REDWARE

by Denise Wilz

Pennsylvania redware platter, 12 inches in length. The design was created using a sgraffito technique then bisque fired to cone 04. Selected areas were then glazed with a green copper oxide glaze then overglazed with a commercial clear glaze and fired to cone 06. *Photos by Lisa Short*

Pennsylvania German folk art found me when I was searching for a different direction to take my clay work. To me this art embodies the spirit of a people who loved life, with their oft-used representations of hearts, tulips, birds and the flower urn. And while the Pennsylvania German potters made mostly plain functional ware with local red earthenware clay, I fell in love with the slip-decorated pieces with their beautiful rich red-and-yellow coloring.

There are basically two styles of decorated Pennsylvania Redware: sgraffito ware and slipware. For ideas to use for decoration, I find inspiration in the Pennsylvania German decorative arts, such as antique redware, fraktur and painted furniture to name just a few sources.

Sgraffito Ware

Sgraffito ware is simply red earthenware decorated with a layer of white slip that is then scratched away to reveal the red clay underneath. To begin, create a form from a slab of clay large enough for your drape mold. Smooth and press the clay to the mold by wiping the surface with a damp sponge, then allow to dry to leather-hard.

The Pennsylvania German potters used upside down bowl-shaped molds carved from wood with a foot underneath, which resembled a mushroom. My drape molds are made of bisque-fired earthenware and I use commercially-made serving bowls as slump molds.

Remove from the platter mold when it is leather hard and place it upright on your work surface or banding wheel. Apply slip with a 2-inch hake brush (figure 1). Brush on two or three thin even coats of slip, making sure the red clay cannot be seen through the surface. (Use a high-quality brush to avoid losing bristles in the slip, which can mar the work.) Clean the edge of excess slip and use a coggle wheel to decorate the edge (figure 2).

Graphic Patterns and Imagery

1. Apply slip with a 2-inch hake brush.

2. Clean the edge of excess slip and use a coggle wheel to decorate the edge.

3. Center the design on the plate and lightly draw over the design with a stylus or pencil.

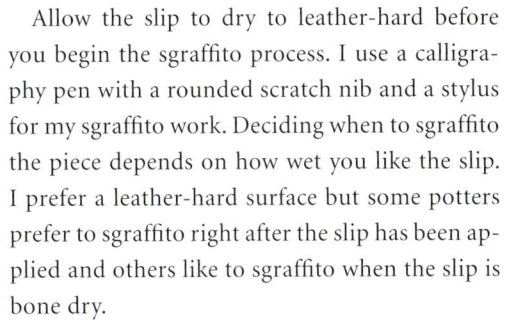

4. Use a sgraffito tool to scratch the design into the slip revealing the red earthenware beneath.

Allow the slip to dry to leather-hard before you begin the sgraffito process. I use a calligraphy pen with a rounded scratch nib and a stylus for my sgraffito work. Deciding when to sgraffito the piece depends on how wet you like the slip. I prefer a leather-hard surface but some potters prefer to sgraffito right after the slip has been applied and others like to sgraffito when the slip is bone dry.

You can use other tools, like a wire-loop tool, sharpened stick or even a pencil in a pinch. As for getting the design onto the plate, it can be freehanded with your sgraffito tool, drawn directly on the slip with a pencil or transferred using tracing paper. To use tracing paper, first draw the design onto the paper, making sure it will fit the size of the plate you are making. Center the design on the plate and lightly draw over the design with a stylus or pencil (figure 3) to leave a slight indentation in the slip as a guide. Then use the sgraffito tool you prefer to scratch the design into the slip revealing the red earthenware beneath (figure 4).

The Pennsylvania German potters applied the glaze directly to the green ware and once-fired the work in a wood-fired kiln. I bisque fire to cone 04, apply a commercial clear glaze then glaze fire to cone 06.

Slip Trailing

Another form of Pennsylvania redware consists of red earthenware decorated with lines and dots of slip. Create a form using the same techniques as described above. To make a smooth surface to work on, lightly wipe the clay with a damp sponge (figure 5). Use a slip cup to draw the design onto the plate (figure 6).

49

Glazing Techniques

5. To make a smooth surface to work on, lightly wipe the clay with a damp sponge.

6. Use a slip cup to draw the design onto the plate.

7. For dots and single lines, use a plastic squeeze bottle.

8. Press the slip into the clay with a rolling pin, wiping the tool after each use in case some slip remained on it.

9. Clean the edge of the plate then decorate the edge with the coggle wheel.

Of course you can use as many straws as you want in your slip cup. The Pennsylvania German potters made their slip cups from small pots that were thrown or pinched with quills inserted as the straws. I've tried making my own clay slip cups but have yet to successfully get the slip to flow out of the quills well evenly enough to look nice, but I'll keep trying. For dots and single lines, I use a plastic squeeze bottle (figure 7).

I find that standing to decorate slipware allows me to move my entire body with the motion of the slip cup across the plate resulting in nice smooth flowing lines.

Allow the slip to dry to the touch then press the slip into the red earthenware with the batter or rolling pin, wiping the tool after each use in case some slip remained on it (figure 8). Clean the edge of the plate to remove any slip that has dripped over the side and then decorate the edge with the coggle wheel (figure 9).

Next, mold the clay by centering the mold upside-down on the clay circle and carefully flip everything over. Press the clay to the mold with your hands; use a batter to tamp the clay down as well.

50

Graphic Patterns and Imagery

10. Tools used to create Pennsylvania slip ware.

11. Slip trailer for creating multiple lines.

Wipe the surface with a damp sponge to smooth and press the clay to the mold. Remove the plate from the mold when it is leather-hard.

Glazing

The leaded glazes the Pennsylvania German potters used gave the slip a warm tint that ranged from almost white to a deep yellow/orange. Instead of using toxic leaded glazes, you can safely emulate the yellowish tint by staining the slip, or by tinting a transparent lead-free glaze with rutile, iron oxide or stains.

There are potters today who continue the tradition of wood-firing lead-glazed ware, but you can use lead-free glazes, electric kilns and plaster or bisque molds. The availability of commercial glazes, clays and stains makes it possible to get consistent results, but you'll need to experiment to get the look you like.

Tools

Tools for making Pennsylvania Redware haven't changed much over the centuries (figure 10). They consisted of a rolling pin, disc cutter and nail, brushes, a sharpened stick for sgraffito, slip cup for slip-trailing, batter, coggle wheel, wooden molds, lead glaze and a wood-fired kiln. Additional glaze colorants included copper oxide for green and manganese for brown/black. And those proficient with throwing used a potter's wheel to create complementary ware and both thrown and handbuilt pieces could be decorated using the same techniques.

Slip Cup

For multiple lines I use a small plastic container with a tight fitting lid (figure 11). I cut three small-diameter drinking straws to about 2 inches in length, and insert them in a straight line approximately 1 inch from the top, with about ¼ inch of the straw inside the container. I apply glue around each hole to seal it and tape the straws together on the outside so they are always the same distance apart, otherwise they'll move while you're using it. Trim the outside straw ends so they're all the same length.

Fill the container with slip that is thin enough to pour from the straws but not too fast. Replace the lid and test the consistency. Make straight and/or wavy lines since both of these designs have been found on antique plates.

An example of slip-trailed redware done in the Pennsylvania German pottery tradition.

51

Graphic Patterns and Imagery
BLACK ON WHITE MIMBRES DECORATION

by Tracy Gamble

Mimbres–style vessel with contemporary silhouette of *Bob the Wonder Dog*, 8½ inches in height. Earthenware with white opaque matt glaze and single coat of gloss black decoration fired to cone 04. Photos by David L. Gamble

The Mimbres people painted images in black on a white background, mostly on earthenware bowls. Very little beyond pottery has been recovered to learn more about these people, so making an interpretation of the Mimbres culture based on archaeological finds remains highly speculative. What is agreed upon, however, is that, between 550 and 1150 C.E., they lived in a 46-mile-long valley in a southwest corner of New Mexico. With no known incidence of war, these peaceful village dwellers also farmed, hunted and foraged. What is also agreed upon is that they painted on pottery, creating images of human figures with rabbits, lizards, fish, antelopes and even bugs from their landscape. It is interesting that Europe was rife with violence, war and religious imagery depicting agonies awaiting the damned in Hell during the same period that the Mimbres were painting images that appear to me to reflect a world viewed as an amiable cosmic circus.

I created a line of pottery celebrating the ancient art of the Mimbres people using their 900-year-old decorative motifs. These individually thrown and hand-painted, earthenware vessels are food, microwave and dishwasher safe for everyday appreciation of Mimbres artistry. The bowl form and antelope decoration of the vessels in the photographic examples was inspired directly from an authentic Mimbres piece in the Eiteljorg Museum collection in Indianapolis, Indiana. There are many images in traditional Mimbres decoration and some of those also appear on this line of pottery, such as the antelope, bird, lizard, fish and rabbit.

Graphic Patterns and Imagery

1. Using your template, trace the image onto the base glaze with a pencil.

2. Add the details, pencil marks will disappear during the kiln firing.

3. Using a small bamboo brush, paint the image with one coat of black, low-fire majolica glaze.

4. Center the vessel on a banding wheel and add lines on and near the rim on the inside using a dagger brush.

5. Mark the centers of the small triangles that will go all the way around the rim.

6. Fill in triangles to complete the motif.

In my recent work, this Mimbres decorative style has progressed into more silhouette-type images from contemporary themes. For example, animal silhouettes—from dogs to chickens—as the main image on a vessel with Mimbres traditional rim designs are used. It's rewarding to celebrate ancient Mimbres artistry by making it new again on today's clay.

Research Mimbres designs on the internet by Googling "Mimbres designs." You'll find several sites with designs that will help you get started. You can also create contemporary designs in the Mimbres style. The antelope is a drawing based on original Mimbres imagery, which was photocopied to a size that best fit the vessel being glazed, then cut out with an X-Acto knife.

The Mimbres decoration is black on white. After bisque firing earthenware clay to cone 03, paint on three coats of an opaque white matt glaze for the white base/background. Apply the glaze one

Glazing Techniques

Mimbres–style lizard and rabbit vessels, wheel-thrown, earthenware, fired to cone 04, by Tracy Gamble.

coat at a time and allow it to dry naturally between coats. Do not dry the coats with a hair dryer or heat gun since the heat shrinks the glaze quickly, causing it to separate from the clay and crawl during firing.

Use a soft lead pencil to trace a design on the white glaze base, then paint on the decoration using black glaze. If you use a gloss black, just a single coat will work if you want to keep the matt or satin effect of the white glaze. A second coat makes the black too glossy. Find a combination of clay and glazes you want to use and test them before investing a lot of time in decorating a piece. I've used various earthenware clay bodies and a variety of low-fire opaque matt white glazes and black glazes, all with good results.

Once the decoration was painted on, the vessel was final glaze fired to cone 04.

Mimbres–style antelope bowls ranging from 3 to 9 inches in diameter, wheel-thrown, red earthenware, fired to cone 04.

Graphic Patterns and Imagery
MAJOLICA IMAGERY

by Jake Allee

When working with majolica glaze techniques, look to historical pieces from Iznik, as well as Spain and Italy. Jake Allee adopted a limited color palette of analogous and complementary combinations for his plates.

The direct nature of applying color through the majolica technique has a nice appeal because the fired result looks pretty close to the way it was applied. For the type of imagery I'm trying to achieve, I've found that simple, refined forms with smooth surfaces are best, but thinking outside of the box might lead you beyond the conventional interpretation of this technique.

Applying the Base Glaze
The majolica technique begins with applying an opaque white glaze over your bisque fired clay. I mix my own clay, but also use APS Red from New Mexico Clay. Any cone 04 red clay that works with your glaze base is suitable.

Linda Arbuckle's majolica glaze base works great (see recipe on page 109), but pay attention to the thickness of the glaze when applying it. If it's too thick, it tends to crawl, and if applied too thin it will cause the surface to be dry. For best results, use tongs to dip the pieces and avoid getting finger marks on them, which become very evident when applying the stains. Any drips can be smoothed out with your finger tip after the glaze completely dries on the bisque piece. Use a dust mask when smoothing the dry glaze.

If you don't want to mix your own glaze, many commercial low-fire white glazes will work just as well including Amaco's LG-11 white low-fire glaze and Laguna's EM-2118 Majolica Glaze. Many other stiff white glazes may also work, just do some tests prior to getting started.

Preparing Stains
To prepare the colors, I mix Gerstley borate with commercial stains from Standard Ceramics Supply, including but not limited to K-44 Royal Purple glaze stain, and #496 Christmas Red glaze stain. The Gerstley borate helps the stains to flux and adding 20% of it works great for most stains, although I add 50% to black stain and 40% to chrome green. I measure ingredients by volume using a plastic

Glazing Techniques

1. Using the banding wheel, bands of stain are applied on the plate to define the edge of the composition.

2. A light wash applied to the background with a larger brush establishes the upper area of the composition.

3. The same color is established in the mid-ground and foreground working toward a sense of unity through color choice, and a horizon line becomes evident.

tablespoon and always run a couple of test tiles through a glaze firing before committing to mixing large amounts.

Commercially available stain mixes, such as Duncan's Concepts Underglazes are listed as suitable for use with majolica. Linda Arbuckle mentions that some Amaco Velvet Underglazes also work, and many other underglazes may as well. Note: Be sure to test any product you plan to use with your clay and glaze, and under your firing conditions before committing to it fully.

Brushes

I use several sizes of bamboo brushes and small watercolor brushes. One that's long and thin, called an "ex liner" (or "rigger" brush as it's used by watercolor artists to paint the detailed rigging on sailboat images) and another called a "script liner" also used for fine lines and details. You may wish to consider different marks made by brushes such as the flats and fans. Pay attention to possibilities in the types of mark each type of brush can make, and develop your skill with brushes using India ink on paper before committing to the ceramic material.

Applying Stain

Plates have a nice flat surface that can be treated like a canvas or piece of paper. My watercolor training in school has proved quite effective in approaching composition as well as color. A landscape-style composition is a great place to start.

My first attempts at multicolored brush decoration turned out pretty disastrous. After looking at what I liked in many different historical styles, I discovered I was using too many colors. Much of the historical work that appealed to me had a stripped down color scheme and relied on white background to create contrast. Even the math-based Della-Robbia compositions of Italy generally used blue, yellow, and green. Thinking about the color wheel and applying design concepts, I went back to square one and use complementary and analogous combinations and added black for emphasis. Gradations in wash provided variation within this limited palette.

Graphic Patterns and Imagery

Process

Start with sketches so you have most of the composition worked out before you commit.

Simplify your color palette. Too many colors can confuse the eye. Consider using one color with varying degrees of intensity along with black as a good place to start. To become more elaborate with color, use a complementary or analogous color scheme.

Define the borders of your image area. Use a banding wheel to define the image area on plates (figure 1). For other forms, use a light wash to define your boundaries.

Use light washes first and create depth by gradually using more intense application of stain. Use yellow first and black last for the final emphasis of critical points in the composition. Don't forget to use the white of the glaze as your lightest value.

Apply background colors first (figure 2). As you work with each color, move through the composition, filling in areas in the midground and foreground that have the same color (figure 3). Remember to block out areas, leaving them white where light colored foreground imagery overlaps the background. The colored stains are like watercolors. Any marks you make continue to be visible even under layers of other colors. If you plan well, darker lines in the foreground used to develop details and that overlap lighter ones enhance the idea of perspective, as the foreground lines will appear closer (figures 4 and 5).

Work from the top of the form to the bottom to avoid smearing your previous work. If you are decorating a plate, work on the outside edges last (figure 6).

Always remember! If you view your efforts as an experiment and work within the context of learning, you won't set yourself up for failure. Consider a range of outcomes as successful. If you are shooting for something too specific, you probably won't get what you are looking for. The challenge of improvement will ultimately drive you to continue to make work.

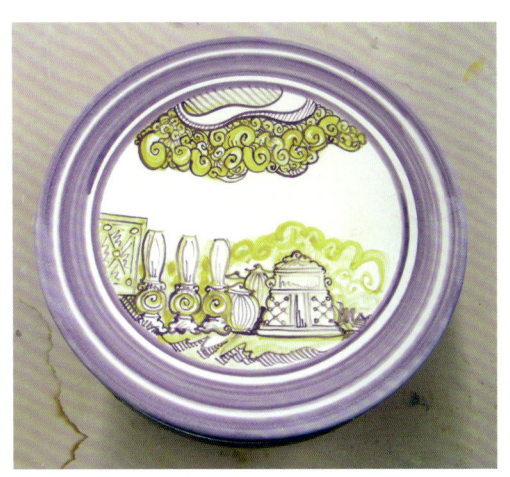

4. Starting back at the top, apply a contrasting color to develop detail using a fine brush.

5. Address the details of the mid- and foreground with the addition of black to create areas of emphasis.

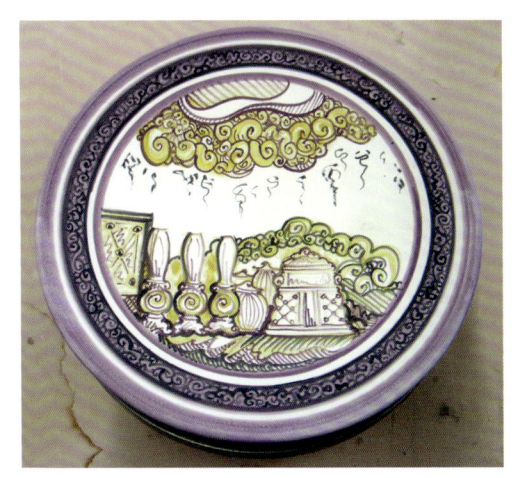

6. A design relating to the rest of the composition is repeated using black in the banded areas.

Graphic Patterns and Imagery
GLAZING PATTERNS

by Frank James Fisher

Nearly every item around my studio or house has the potential to be a glaze applicator, and for every new idea, there is a pile of failed attempts. But hidden in many failures are the seeds of new success; you just need to look at it in the right context.

Three Approaches

Here are three glaze application techniques. The first method is a *direct contact* approach, the second is a *stenciling* approach, and the third is a *transfer* approach.

The direct approach involves dipping an object into glaze (in this case a sponge roller) and pressing the object against the surface. The shape of the object and the action used to apply the glaze determines the type of mark it leaves. The object can be soft and absorbent like a sponge roller or it can be rigid like a kitchen spatula—any object can leave a unique mark.

The stencil approach involves applying glaze through or around another object. This mark is based on a positive versus negative image. The cheese cloth acts as a stencil and the roller is the applicator. After applying the glaze through the cloth, a unique grid of squares is created. Other materials with an open weave, for example, lace curtains, can also be used.

The transfer approach involves selecting a textured object, applying glaze to its raised surface

Household items make can be used in a variety of creative ways to apply glaze. Here are three examples showing direct contact (left) glazed with Warm Jade Green and Licorice Black; stenciling (center) glazed with Shelly's Blue and Licorice Black; and transfer (right) glazed with Warm Jade Green and Licorice Black. All are white stoneware fired in oxidation. See recipes on page 60.

and printing the texture onto the ceramic surface. Any object that has a distinct texture can be used. The glaze is rolled onto the object. The image is transferred by pressing the glazed object against the pot's surface. Bubble wrap (used for shipping) became the transferred texture for this demonstration. The resulting starlike shapes wrap around the surface to form a unique glaze pattern.

Graphic Patterns and Imagery

Set up the roller and pour glaze into the tray.

After absorbing glaze into the sponge roller, dab the glaze in a pattern onto the bottle.

For the stencil approach, apply the base glaze then hold a piece of textured cloth in position on the bottle.

Using a sponge roller, roll the glaze over the textured fabric.

By using everyday objects for these glazing techniques, an entire new world of glaze marks and patterns awaits discovery.

Glazing Tips

- Wipe the your bisqueware before glazing. Fine dust builds up quickly in a studio, and this is true even if the pots were removed immediately from a bisque kiln. Glaze can slide off an unwiped pot onto a kiln shelf during firing.
- Glazing very dry bisque surfaces results in an extra-thick glaze application, because the moisture from the wet glaze is quickly sucked into the dry bisque causing a thick layer of glaze to adhere. Wipe the surface before glazing for a thinner glaze layer, but be careful not to soak the bisque or leave standing water.
- The best sponges for glazing are the large wallpaper sponges sold at building supply stores. These sponges have small pores and are excellent for wiping wet glaze off pots. A large-pore sponge doesn't last as long and leaves uneven edges when wiping a glazed surface.
- If you need to wipe glaze off your pot, do it immediately while the glaze is still wet. Wet glaze comes off easier and quicker and causes less staining than if you waited until the glaze was dry on the pot.

Glazing Techniques

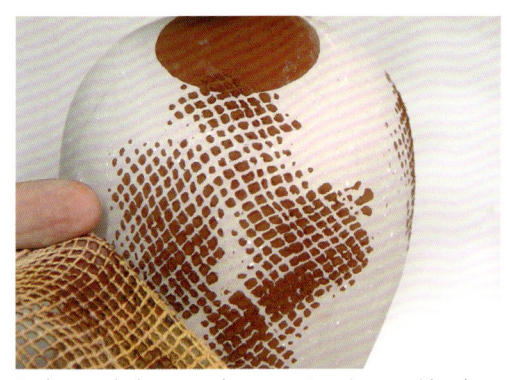

Peel away cloth to reveal texture. Experiment with other materials such as lace, nylon window screen, etc.

Transfer a pattern like bubble wrap. Roll the glaze onto the domed pills. of the bubble wrap.

Roll your form across the glazed bubble wrap.

The completed glazed texture wraps around the entire form. At this point, dip the bottle top quickly into a second overlapping glaze if you want.

WARM JADE GREEN
Cone 6

Whiting	16 %
Ferro Frit 3124	9
Talc	9
Custer Feldspar	40
EPK Kaolin	10
Silica	16
	100 %
Add: Copper Carbonate	4 %
Rutile	6 %

LICORICE BLACK
Cone 6

Whiting	4 %
Ferro Frit 3134	26
Custer Feldspar	22
Talc	5
EPK Kaolin	17
Silica	26
	100 %
Add: Cobalt Carbonate	2 %
Red Iron Oxide	9 %

SHELLY'S BLUE
Cone 6

by Michelle Bonior

Dolomite	4.0 %
Whiting	6.0
Zinc Oxide	4.0
Custer Feldspar	47.0
Gillespie Borate	13.0
EPK Kaolin	3.0
Silica	23.0
	100.0 %
Add: Rutile	2.0 %
Copper Carbonate	1.5 %
Cobalt Carbonate	0.5 %
Bentonite	2.0 %

For the bottles shown, Warm Jade Green and Shelly's Blue were used as a base glaze with the Licorice Black added as decoration on a white stoneware clay body.

Graphic Patterns and Imagery
POURED DECORATION

by Sam Scott

In the early 1970s, an encounter with Bob Sperry's work influenced my decision to go to the University of Washington. Sperry's on-glaze brushwork had attracted me and after three years there, in addition to facility with a brush and learning to work with porcelain, I had acquired many skills. Upon graduation, I set up my studio and began to develop my own approach to brushwork. One of my techniques was to leave areas of the porcelain surface unglazed. When I applied the oxides, I would get a different color depending on whether the brushwork was on clay or glaze. I applied the glaze by pouring it over selective areas, and with practice, I began to control the poured areas and was able create interesting patterns. The biomorphic shapes would widen or taper based on the flow of the glaze and the form of the piece being glazed.

As time passed, the patterns became more interesting, but given that I used a clear glaze, there was little contrast to the clay and glaze. My main focus was to add visual interest to the brushwork. In the 1990s, I began to develop a black matte glaze. Because this black glaze contrasted with the white porcelain, the patterns themselves became the main focus of the surface decoration.

Making a Splash

Once the piece is bisque-fired to cone 09, it is ready to be glazed. All of my forms are smooth with uninterrupted curves, making surface decoration a bit easier. Whether I use brushwork or the pouring

Lidded jar, 14 inches (36 cm) in height, wheel-thrown porcelain, black glaze.

technique, throwing lines or variations in surface texture compete with and alter the decoration.

The technique I use is remarkably simple. I use a small, flexible margarine container with a thin edge so I can alter its width as needed to get a wider or narrower flow. As I begin to apply the glaze, it is a combination of pour and splash (figure 1). If I touch the container to the pot, it splits the flow of glaze. If I just splash it on the piece, I am not able to control the shape as the glaze flows down the surface. The angle at which I hold the pot, the shape of the piece, the viscosity of the glaze, and the degree of impetus I give the glaze at the initial pour all factor into the shapes that develop (figures 2 and 3). I also alter the angle and directional-

Glazing Techniques

ity (from the rim or from the foot) of the pours to create a graphic tension on the surface.

I pour from either the top or bottom in a fairly random manner to begin with. Once this area is dry, I pour from the other direction, reacting to the shapes that now exist on the surface, as shown in figures 2 and 3. At this point, I can see the pattern begin to energize the surface. The size of the biomorphic shapes, the distance between the shapes, whether they touch or not, all factor into the effect. When I am finished pouring, I scrape off the inevitable small splatters with a needle tool and use an eraser to clean off any residue. Because of the fluidity of the poured shapes, I rarely alter them. If I get an edge I don't like, I pour over that area to clean it up.

1. Apply the glaze using a combination of pouring and splashing from a flexible plastic container.

2. The shape of the pot, glaze viscosity, velocity and angling the pot changes the poured shape.

3. The finished pot, prior to glaze firing. Glaze was poured with the pot upside down as well as upright.

Black and white vase, 10 inches (25 cm) in height, wheel-thrown and handbuilt porcelain, black glaze.

Graphic Patterns and Imagery
SARAH JAEGER'S BOTANICAL PATTERNS

by Emily Donahoe

Geometric patterns and forms combine with organic, plant-inspired lines in Sarah Jaeger's inviting functional pots. In her hands, a modest, wheel-thrown serving bowl becomes something special with some easy alterations and a layered, wax-resist glazing technique.

The alterations developed over years of playing around with simple geometric forms—dividing up the space, making rounds into squares, and just seeing where things went.

"A lot of the evolution just comes from working on the wheel and doing something and then thinking, well, what would happen if I tried this?" she explains. "So it doesn't start out as high concept all the time."

Sarah says that the alterations are "both visual and tactile—and both of those things come into play with functional pots." Add to that Sarah's love of decoration and the surface of the bowl becomes a space where pattern and irregularity meet. She says her goal is to make a bowl that functions well, that's also beautiful and adds some joy and a sense of festivity to someone's meal.

Glazing Process

Sarah works atop the New York Times Arts and Travel sections—after she's read the articles, of course. She wears latex gloves to protect her hands from the abrasive glaze. After waxing the foot of the bisque-fired bowl with paraffin, she uses tongs to dip the bowl into a clear glaze, allowing it to dry for a bit before beginning the first step in decorating.

"This is another one of my secret tools: it's a no. 2 pencil," Sarah explains as she draws a simple leaf pattern inside the bowl (figure 1), and then uses a paintbrush to fill in the patterns with a wash of rutile and Gerstley borate. She applies a thin layer for a translucent, cloudy effect.

Glazing Techniques

1. Draw a design on the inside of the freshly glazed pot using a pencil.

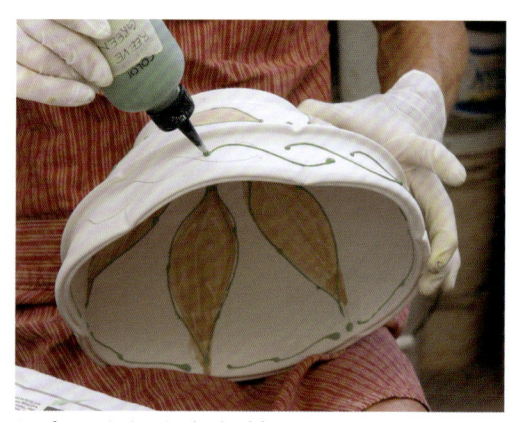

2. After painting in the leaf forms using a colored wash, trail on green glaze line decorations.

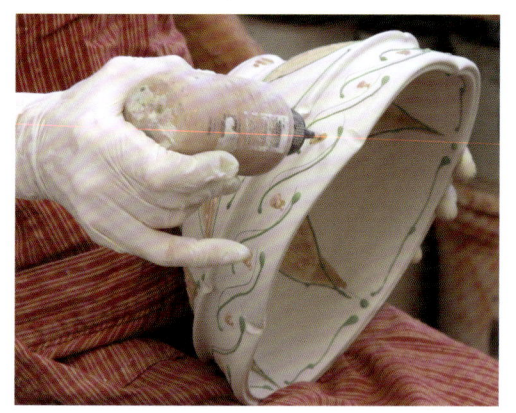

3. Additional red glaze decorations are trailed on next. The trailed glaze should be thicker so it does not run.

4. Use a tinted wax resist to visibly protect the painted and trailed patterns and shapes.

5. After the wax dries, paint a layer of wash, here copper sulfate, over the surface to create another layer.

As she works, Sarah explains that her decorations have evolved out of hand repetition and "responding to the curve of the pot."

"A lot of my glaze decorations started out as very geometric patterns and over the years evolved into more botanical patterns. The longer I did it . . . the more organic the lines and the forms and those decorative motifs became," says Sarah. "I like patterns that are pretty organized and symmetrical but then, when the pot gets fired everything softens and relaxes. There's a kind of nice contradiction there."

The next two glazes are applied in thick, dense lines. The first is Reeve Green, mixed very thick to give the bowl some texture (figure 2). Sarah applies the glaze using Clairol color applicator bottles, which she gets at a beauty supply store. She then uses the same technique with an orange-red glaze, which is made from the same base glaze as Reeve Green, but with red inclusion stain added (figure 3). On the outside of the bowl, Sarah uses the same elements in a different arrangement; she decorates the bowl all the way down to the underside of the foot, filling in the spots between leaves with simple waves and crosshatches.

"It's a three-dimensional pot," says Sarah. "I think it matters to pay attention to all of it." Plus," she adds, "when people wash dishes, they love that the undersides are decorated. One time this guy in California emailed me a photo of bowls in the dishwasher."

Wax and Wash

Wax resist is an old technique, but Sarah finds that she uses it a little bit differently than most potters.

"One thing that caused me to keep playing with this technique is that I really love surfaces that have a sense of depth," says Sarah. "It confuses that figure-ground relationship—and for some reason that confusion really interests me."

Sarah uses a color-tinted Aftosa wax to go over the decorations on the bowl with a Japanese-style brush (figure 4). This type of wax helps her to see what she's done and also brushes on more easily than paraffin wax.

"The wax will repel anything that goes on over it. Some other waxes that flow and brush well don't seem to resist the cobalt sulfate as well as Aftosa," explains Sarah. "So I will paint with wax on all the parts of this that I want to remain what they are now."

Sarah's final step is to brush a cobalt sulfate wash over the entire bowl (figure 5). She mixes the colorant with water by eye, testing it on newsprint to see that it is the right concentration before applying it. Sarah explains, "The form of cobalt sulfate that I use, because it's water-soluble, you get a really soft line. Just like when a watercolor goes on paper and it bleeds into the paper, as the water of the cobalt sulfate wash evaporates, the cobalt bleeds into the glaze, so the line quality is really soft."

CAUTION: Cobalt sulfate, like all soluble salts is easily absorbed into the skin. It is important to wear latex gloves when working with this, or any other soluble salt colorant. It is not recommended to use this material in group studio situations.

As she finishes up the pot, Sarah reflects on the paradox of spending so much time discussing technique—and so much time decorating a single pot. "At the end, you don't want the person who is using the pot to think about technique at all. You don't want it to look like it was a lot of work; you just want it to look like itself."

REEVE BASE
Cone 10 (oxidation or reduction)

Custer Feldspar	75 %
Whiting	15
EPK Kaolin	5
Silica	5
	100 %
Add: Bentonite	2 %
Green: Chrome Oxide	4 %
Red: Cerdec Intensive Red	10 %

Used as the trailing overglaze colors. When trailing this glaze, it needs to be thick so that it does not run.

LIMESTONE CLEAR
Cone 10 (oxidation or reduction)

Custer Feldspar	27.0 %
Ball Clay (OM 4)	14.0
EPK Kaolin	7.0
Whiting	20.5
Silica	31.5
	100.0 %

This glaze is not an absolute clear. On its own in reduction, it's a little greenish.

Graphic Patterns and Imagery
FUMIYA MUKOYAMA'S ZOGAN YUSAI

by Naomi Tsukamoto

Inlaid geometric slip and glaze designs inspired by the sun, waves and sea spray give Fumiya Mukoyama's works individual character.

Japan is filled with pottery and potters, and traditionally their styles have been regionally classified. If you are a young ceramic artist living in one of these kamamoto (literally translated as "by the kiln") towns, your challenge is to break out of the tradition and become recognized for your own style. Fumiya Mukoyama lives and works in the Mashiko region, where Mingei is their signature style. For many years, he has practiced to perfect the zogan yusai technique on his wave and geometric patterns. Zogan means inlaid, and yusai means coloring with glazes. Having been trained in Kyoto as a tea ware maker, his forms are extremely precise and pristine. But the patterns he creates and the combinations of glazes and stains he paints add warmth and organic tones to his forms. When asked how he got into this highly technical and meticulous surface design, he said it started with the sea spray he saw at dawn. In order to paint the sun, waves, and the ocean with glazes, he began using an inlaid technique to emphasize the separation of colors. Here he created a typical Japanese rice bowl to demonstrate his one-of-a-kind zogan yusai technique.

Drafting and Etching Design

Trim a piece from the bottom all the way to the lip of the bowl, both to remove excess clay and to remove throwing lines and create a smooth surface. In order for the inlaid design to come out clearly, it is important to make the surface as smooth as possible at this stage. Mukoyama ends the trimming by going over the surface with a sponge, erasing all the trimming lines. Finer clay

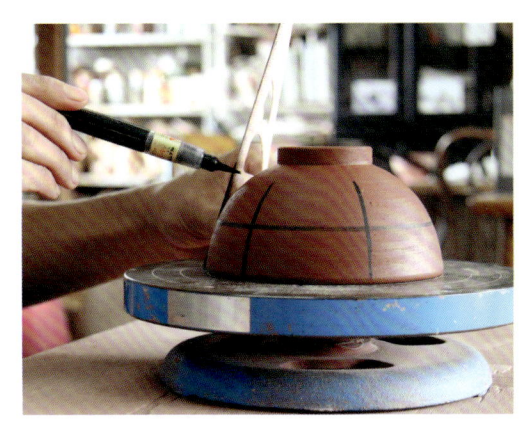

Graphic Patterns and Imagery

1. Draw drafting lines with calligraphy ink, dividing the surface into vertical and horizontal sections.

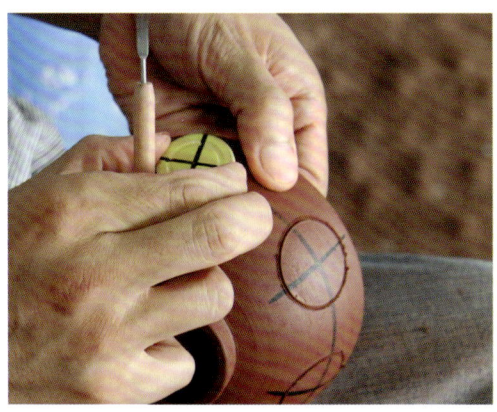

2. Create a circular incised shape in the surface of the bowl using a medicine bottle top or other tool.

3. Etch or incise the dotted lines using a fabric rotary cutter or pizza cutter.

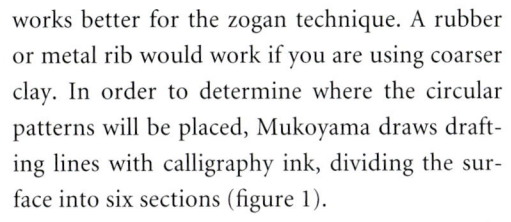

4. Use a soft brush to lightly pat the kaolin slip into the pattern of incised lines and dots (figure 10).

works better for the zogan technique. A rubber or metal rib would work if you are using coarser clay. In order to determine where the circular patterns will be placed, Mukoyama draws drafting lines with calligraphy ink, dividing the surface into six sections (figure 1).

The tools used to create geometric shapes do not have to be fancy. Here a medicine cap is used for the circular pattern (figure 2). The lines on the cap help him to line up the circle vertically and horizontally with the lines drawn on his pot. Clean and round the edges with a trimming tool after etching the design. After making the etched lines smooth, go over the lines with the needle tool to round inside of the lines. A fabric rotary cutter (or pizza cutter) is used to etch the dotted lines (figure 3).

Zogan

Because the slip is only inlaid inside the lines, Mukoyama uses watered down pure Amakusa Porcelain Stone powder, which is equivalent to Cornwall Stone. This simplifies cleaning the surface later. This slip will not work for painting the surface though, because once dried, it is powdery and will flake off easily.

The slip should be quite watery, much thinner than the normal consistency, in order to fill in the small dots. Use the brush to lightly pat in the slip (figure 4). Once the slip dries, rub in the slip further using your fingertips (figure 5).

Normally, you'd scrape the surface to finish the slip inlay; however, since the slip was pure clay, all you need to do is to wipe off the surface lightly with

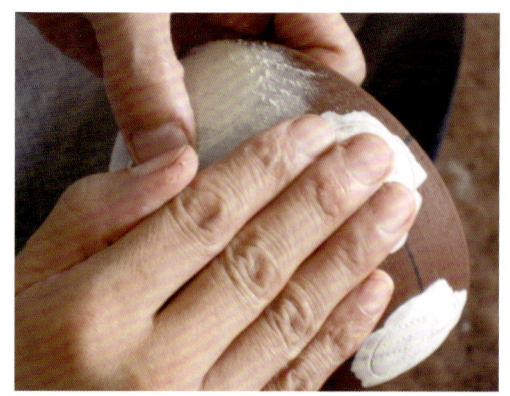

5. Once the slip dries, rub it in to the lines further with your fingers. It will be very powdery once dry.

6. Wipe off the surface lightly with a cheese cloth like fabric. The slip inlay lines show clearly on the surface.

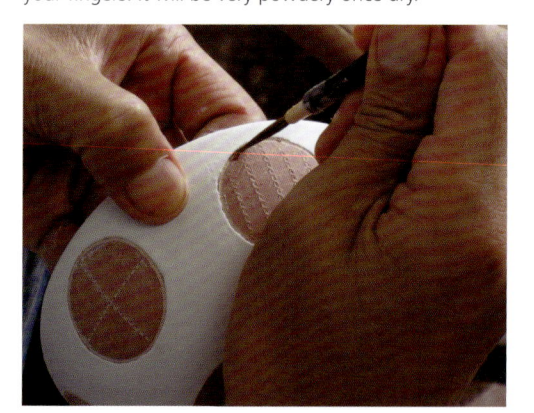

7. After the second bisque firing, mask off the lines within the circular areas so they will remain white.

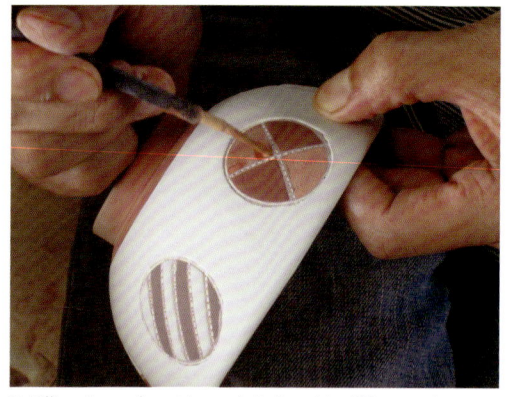

8. Filling in each patterned circle with different glazes, metallic oxides and underglazes.

a cheese cloth like fabric (figure 6). Be cautious not to wipe the surface too hard, otherwise, you will lose the inlaid lines. The more clearly you can maintain the division between the inlay and surrounding surface, the more vivid the final colors will be. After cleaning the surface, bisque fire the piece.

Glazing the Background

Once bisque fired, make sure you clean the ware with a wet sponge first in order to achieve the best glazing result. Brush wax resist on the circular patterns. Mukoyama usually covers the lines with water-based latex resist using a very thin brush first, and then fills inside the design with melted wax mixed with kerosene using a small brush. Using latex on the lines ensures that the resist can be removed and reapplied if it is covering more than just the incised lines and patterned areas.

After the resist dries, glaze the inside by pouring first, then dip the base glaze outside. Wipe any glaze off of the circular design areas and clean any drips on the foot ring before the second bisque firing. The purpose of the second bisque firing is to burn off the resist and to fire on the base glaze.

Yusai

After the second bisque, only mask off the lines (figure 7). You will want to fill in the rest of the area using colorants and glazes. Because some glazes do run, it works better if you mask a little over the lines rather than precisely covering only the lines.

Fill in each pattern with different glazes, metallic oxides, and underglazes. Mukoyama only uses two colors for each pattern to achieve the unified balance (figure 8). You could also leave some parts bare to take advantage of the clay color. Glaze from lighter to darker colors as you work to keep them from contaminating one another.

This is the last glazing step. Think of glazes and stains as colors and carefully consider the color balance for each circular pattern and between the patterns. Also consider the type of finish (glossy, matte, and dry) you combine. Depending on how you combine the linear patterns and colors, you will find numerous design possibilities in zogan yusai.

Left to right: imari gosu cobalt pigment and iron matte glaze; red underglaze and white matte glaze; and titanium dioxide and iron glaze.

Left to right: Imari gosu cobalt pigment and white matte glaze; bengala iron pigment and titanium glaze; and iron glaze and white matte glaze.

Graphic Patterns and Imagery

CLAY

Shigaraki Namikoshi Stoneware 100%
Add: Bengala Iron Pigment 2%
      Manganese Dioxide 2%

INLAID SLIP

Amakusa Porcelain Stone 100%

Mix with water until thinned

WHITE MATTE GLAZE

Fukushima Feldspar. 57.0%
Gray Limestone 31.5
Ball Clay 11.5
                                                  100.0%

Add: Zirconium Silicate 10.3%

IRON MATT GLAZE

Fukushima Feldspar. 57.0%
Gray Limestone 31.5
Ball Clay 11.5
                                                  100.0%

Add: Bengala Iron Pigment 1.0%
      Manganese Dioxide 0.3%

TITANIUM GLAZE

Fukushima Feldspar 65.0
Gray Limestone. 8.0
Titanium Dioxide. 14.6
Zinc Oxide. 12.4
                                                  100.0%

IRON GLAZE

Clear Glaze. 100.0%
Add: Bengala Iron Pigment 7.5%
      Manganese Dioxide 2.0%

SUBSTITUTIONS

Use the following substitutions for the Japanese glaze materials. Test all substitutions and adjust as needed.
Shigaraki Namikoshi Stoneware: Substitute Fine Grog White Stoneware
Amakusa Porcelain Stone: Substitute Cornwall Stone
Fukushima Feldspar: Substitute Custer Feldspar
Gray Limestone: Substitute Whiting
Bengala Iron Pigment: Substitute Red Iron Oxide

PIGMENTS FOR GEOMETRIC PATTERNS

Imari Gosu Cobalt Pigment (Gosu is a commercially available product in Japan. Where this is not available, substitute Cobalt Carbonate or blue Mason Stains.)
Bengala Iron Pigment
High Fire Red Underglaze
Titanium Dioxide

3

Creating Layers and Depth
USING GRAVITY TO ENHANCE A SURFACE

by Kari E. Radasch

Dinner plate, terra cotta with White Slip and Kari's Best Transparent Glaze.

It is a shallow notion to insist that low-fire work lacks the glaze depth that stoneware and porcelains claim to have. On the contrary, it is as much the case that high-fire work lacks the glaze depth of terra cotta. There are many reasons for this misconception, but the most preeminent one, in my opinion, is that our low-fire vocabulary is not as developed as our high-fire one. We will begin to fix that right here.

Surface is more than a seductive veneer; at its best it engages the clay. My surfaces begin from the minute I touch the clay, with the rolling out of coils, the pounding out of slabs and the pinching of forms. I embrace spontaneous yet purposeful marks—brush trails, glaze drips and thinly applied slips. I try to embed as much information as possible in the making so that the glaze can respond accordingly. These marks have a huge impact on the finished glaze surface. They aid in building layers and provide a variety of terrain and textures to which the glazes respond. These marks are not only functional, but they tell a story. They recall motions and actions of the maker. This veneer adds another layer of surface and meaning.

I work with a terra cotta to which I add 2–4% red iron oxide and burnt umber. I do this for two reasons: to encourage an active interface between the clay and glaze, and to make the clay rich and chocolaty. I use terra-cotta clay because of its robust nature, its visual weight, the way it records a surface and the way it responds to my touch. I begin by making marks such as fingerprints, incisions, tracings, inscriptions and serrations from a

Glazing Techniques

1. After using a pencil to divide and mark the areas for the different glazes, I brush the bisqueware with a copper carbonate wash over all of the slip-trailed and textured surfaces.

2. I wipe the copper carbonate off, allowing it to be trapped in the piped slip and sprigged buttons. Since it is a strong flux, it increases the melt, encouraging the glazes to run and pool over these slip barriers.

3. Glazes that run the most are brushed on, then stiffer glazes are piped out of a syringe. For example, two transparent gloss glazes—tinted to have amber and pink tones—are brushed into the demarcated pencil areas. Then pink majolica is applied (using a syringe) on top

4. Finally, for added insurance, I will encourage specific areas of glaze to melt by adding copper carbonate wash on top of the glaze. This combination of stiff and fluid glazes, along with gravity, provided the effects I desire.

rib. Next, I may emboss areas of the slab with architectural motifs reminiscent of decorative tile and tin ceiling panels. I then place a heavy white slip over the entire piece using a large mop brush, topping it off with a much thicker slip piped through a syringe. The final wet step is attaching candy-like buttons made from a thickened version of the white slip. One of my first important realizations was that I needed to use glazes with different melting points. Their differing viscosities gives them dimension and prevents them from looking too shiny or flat. After hundreds of glaze tests using several standard glazes (transparent gloss, satin white opaque and majolica), I began layering and floating glazes upon one another. I ended up choosing a majolica because of its thick, stiff marshmallowy looking qualities, and two different transparent gloss glazes (one

Creating Layers and Depth

that is accepting of stains and another that is a barium-fritted glaze, reminiscent of those luscious lead glazes).

I also started paying close attention to gravity, watching how glazes move, melt and flow depending upon their mass, temperature and location on the pot. I have found two things that help my glazes flow better during application: I add both CMC Gum (0.6%) for brushability and Veegum T (1.6–1.8%, depending on how heavily the glaze is fritted) for suspension. I also have found that spraying each pot with a mist of water (aside from washing the bisque before glazing) not only lessens the pinholes but acts as a provisional vehicle that assists in achieving an even, flowing first glaze coat.

I have no doubt that the most consistent method of firing is to use pyrometric cones. I have learned this through experience. Firing with cones ensures that your results will be as true as possible. However, some of my more important aesthetic decisions have been based on firing mistakes. One of these mistakes led to my decision to fire to a soft cone 02. Raising my firing temperature is the final step in encouraging my glazes to move more than they would at cone 04. The added benefits are a stronger clay and glaze interface, and a more vitreous clay body.

CAUTION: Limited exposure to copper is considered relatively safe; however, copper carbonate is a heavy metal, so to be safe, I always wear latex gloves when wiping off the copper wash.

Large serving platter, 20 inches in length, terra cotta with White Slip and Kari's Best Transparent Glaze.

Glazing Techniques

WHITE SLIP
Cone 04–02

Talc	40.0 %
Nepheline Syenite	10.0
Ball Clay	40.0
Silica	10.0
	100.0 %
Add: Zircopax	7.0 %

KARI'S BEST TRANSPARENT GLAZE
Cone 04–02

Gerstley Borate	11.0 %
Talc	30.0
Pemco Frit P-626	19.0
Ferro Frit 3124	11.0
Spodumene	14.0
EPK Kaolin	15.0
	100.0 %
Add: Wollastonite	5.0 %
Veegum T	1.0 %
CMC Gum	0.4 %

Celadon
Copper Carbonate . . . . 0.3 %

Blue
Cobalt Carbonate . . . . 1.5 %
Copper Carbonate . . . . 2.0 %

Grape
Manganese Dioxide . . . . 7.0 %
Copper Carbonate . . . . 0.5 %

Emerald Green
Copper Carbonate . . . . 6.0 %

WOODY HUGHES BASE
Cone 04–02

Gerstley Borate	26.0 %
Lithium Carbonate	4.0
Nepheline Syenite	20.0
Ferro Frit 3124	30.0
EPK Kaolin	10.0
Silica	10.0
	100.0 %
Add: Veegum T	1.6 %
CMC Gum	0.5 %

For soft color that will remain transparent, add 7% stain.

MAJOLICA
Cone 04–02

Ferro Frit 3124	66.3 %
Ferro Frit 3110	15.9
Ferro Frit 5301	0.5
EPK Kaolin	17.3
	100.0 %
Add: Zircopax	15.9 %
Veegum T	1.6 %
CMC Gum	0.5 %

For soft color, add 7% stain.

Note: CMC is an organic gum and will break down over time (not only will it stop working, but it has the potential to develop an odor). When left to dry, CMC creates a hard glaze coat, which is great if it is necessary to transport your wares, but when left in a brush, the gum will act like a glue—sticking the bristles together, making it tough to wash out.

Detail of large serving platter

Creating Layers and Depth
LAYERED DECORATION

by Adero Willard

A primary creative idea behind my decoration techniques is manipulating real or illusory depth through relationships between different textures, patterns, colors, and proportions. Using different techniques and tools on the same piece adds to the contrast. Quilts are one of the many inspirations I draw from. Separate patches create repeating patterns that ultimately become a complete and unified form. Translated to clay and glazes, the patchwork appearance and depth comes from layering of underglazes and the revealing of layers through masking (using wax resist). Using underglazes gives one the immediacy of working with color in painterly ways.

Another important element in my decoration is the role of organic or nature-inspired themes, and their contrast with geometric shapes. Having grown up in a major metropolis, maybe it comes from how I loved the park as a refuge in the city! In my work, I try to create decoration that interrelates with the character of the form. I alter forms on the wheel (and sometimes add handbuilt elements) to introduce the dynamic of asymmetry and to evoke details from textiles, like a ruffle or a seam.

Platter Planning

A larger form like a platter allows more surface for contrasting decoration to inhabit. I create a double lip, and then alter the shape of the form by pulling and stretching the edge to vary the degree to which the two conjoin (figure 1). Consideration of how these alterations affect the character of the form helps inspire the mapping out of the decoration: which areas of decoration will be contained inside the form, which will extend to some, but not all edges, and so on. Using an X-Acto blade, I map out areas so contrasting patterns will collide, intersect, and overlap (figure 2). It may be helpful to make a separate sketch on paper and keep it nearby in case you lose track of the order of the layers during the application of underglazes.

1. Throw and alter a platter form on the wheel, stretching the clay to create decorative and asymmetrical edges.

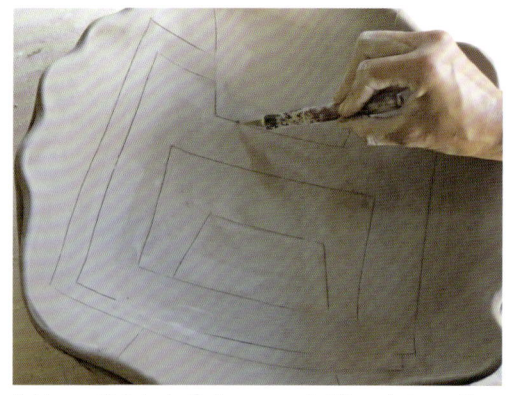

2. Use an X-Acto knife to map out different decoration areas. You may want to make a separate sketch on paper for reference.

3. Leaving areas bare, apply black underglaze as background color. Paint shapes with wax resist to create the first layer of pattern.

4. Apply white underglaze to the entire surface. Once dry, retrace your decoration map.

Layers and Masking

I apply a layer of black underglaze once the form is leather hard. I leave the clay body exposed in specific places based on my decoration map. The next step is to introduce the first wax-resist element once the underglaze is dry to the touch (figure 3). Here, leaf shapes are painted onto the surface using wax. If you haven't worked with masking, you may find it helpful to think of applying wax as preserving whatever is directly underneath it, even as more underglaze is applied. The first pattern I create uses relatively large shapes, which will appear as black-on-clay-body. When the wax is dry, the entire surface is covered in white underglaze (figure 4). When that layer is dry to the touch, I use a dry sponge to remove the underglaze that beads up on the waxed areas to prevent glaze defects (repeat this after every application of underglaze to a waxed area).

Creating Patterns with Sgraffito

At this point I use the X-Acto blade to retrace the lines of my map, as the underglaze may obscure them. The next decoration I apply using sgraffito. I use the side edge of the tip of the blade, carving away the upper white layer to reveal the black layer beneath. In some areas, I create a vine pattern, which sweeps and loops around itself and between the mapped-out areas, echoing the waved edge of the altered form (figure 5). I also use sgraffito to begin a pattern of a contrasting geometric style in adjoining areas (figure 6). Note: Clear away the dust created by the carved underglaze with a dry brush;

Creating Layers and Depth

5. Using the side edge of an X-Acto blade, create sgraffito decoration. The ivy pattern accentuates the platter's irregular edges.

6. Create a contrasting, geometrical sgraffito pattern in adjoining areas, per your map. Clear away shavings with a dry brush.

7. In one area of the ivy pattern, use cross-hatching to make the ivy decoration dark-on-light (positive space).

don't clear it by blowing it away, as it's harmful to inhale. I like to create contrasting dimension in a piece by alternating between carving the positive shape of the vine in some areas, and carving away the negative space in others (figures 7–8).

Variations on Technique

Recall that some areas had no black underneath the white underglaze: these will show as white-on-clay-body, where the rest will show as white-over-black. (The thickness of the white layer determines how dark or light the resulting combination will be.) In the area with white-on-clay-body, I use a slip-trailing bottle to create decoration that is suggestive of writing without being overly literal (figure 9). This black design element contrasts with the larger black leaf shapes created by the initial wax application.

8. In the other areas, cross-hatch around the ivy to create a light-on-dark decoration (negative space).

Second Resist Layer

With the sgraffito and slip-trail decoration complete, I apply the next wax decoration to preserve elements at this level before applying more colors of underglaze. Between the large leaf shapes preserved by the first layer of resist, I add a second vine-like pattern using wax (figure 10). Over the grid, I introduce a corresponding geometric element of wax circles that accentuates the curvilinear aspects of the form (figure 11). The wax also serves purely as a mask to preserve areas where the decoration is complete.

Glazing Techniques

9. Use a slip-trailing bottle to decorate the bare area, contrasting delicate strokes against larger bold elements.

10. Apply a second ivy pattern with wax resist. Although constrained within the map, this creates the appearance of endless flow.

11. The second wax pattern contrasts by its geometric nature, as well as contrasting circles against the sgraffito grid.

12. Apply yellow underglaze in the gridded areas. Remove any underglaze that beads up on the waxed areas with a dry sponge.

Expanding the Palette

I introduce other colors at this point; areas masked by wax will not be affected. Using wax as a mask protects against the brush slipping or drips. Use a dry sponge to remove the underglaze that beads up on the wax after every step. The geometric area has two layers of color; the first is yellow-over-white, with the wax circles showing through the yellow (figure 12). Then, I apply a third level of resist over parts of the yellow, introducing a spiral that relates geometrically but contrasts in scale and gesture (figure 13). The organic area will have red-over-white, with the brush-applied vine showing through the red (figure 14). Once the wax spirals dry, the white-over-yellow layer, with the spirals showing through the white, completes the geometric area (figure 15).

Two Firings

The platter must be bisque fired before glazing. After the initial firing, I use a non-stick-pan scrubbing pad to sand off the flaky residue that the wax leaves behind, then I dunk the entire piece in glaze to seal the decoration and make the colors more vivid. I glaze fire to cone 03 in an electric kiln.

Materials and Recipes

I use terra cotta from Sheffield Pottery in Massachusetts. I coat the interiors of my vessels with Bill's Basic Liner glaze and cover the exteriors with Pete Pinnell's consistent and reliable clear glaze.

For underglaze, I use Spectrum's 501 White, Amaco's V309-Deep Yellow, LUG-1 Black, V383-Light Red, and their V387-Bright Red.

Creating Layers and Depth

13. A second wax pattern, also geometric but similar in character to the ivy, is applied over the yellow underglaze.

14. Apply red underglaze to the second ivy area. The wax decoration will show through. Remove any underglaze that beads up on the wax with a dry sponge.

BILL'S BASIC LINER GLAZE
Cone 04–2

Ferro Frit 3124	65.8 %
Kona F-4 Feldspar	17.1
Nepheline Syenite	6.3
6 Tile Clay	10.8
	100.0 %
Add: Bentonite	2.0 %
Rutile	0.5 %
Zircopax	14.0 %

Use less Zircopax for a less-opaque white liner glaze. I use 10%. Substitute Minspar 200 for Kona F-4 feldspar.

PETE PINNELL CLEAR
Cone 04–2

Magnesium Carbonate	10 %
Ferro Frit 3195	73
EPK Kaolin	10
Silica	7
	100 %
Add: Bentonite	2.0 %
For Amber Tones	
Add: Nickel Carbonate	0.5–1.0%
For Aqua to Turquoise Green	
Add: Copper Oxide	0.5–2.0%

This glaze fires as high as cone 2 with good results.

15. Apply a layer of white underglaze over the yellow. Remove any underglaze that beads up on the waxed areas with a dry sponge.

When I use a variety of decoration techniques on forms with greater dimensionality, such as a lidded jar, the interplay and contrast are both revealed and disguised.

Creating Layers and Depth
COMBINING CLAY, STAIN AND GLAZE

by Marty Fielding

Pitchers are one of the forms in the pottery canon that compel me the most, and the challenge they put forth is quite enticing. Since I work predominantly on the wheel, that challenge starts with throwing a tall and shapely piece that is voluminous and lightweight. The final form is a wheel-thrown and slab-built combination I finish off with terra sigillata, underglaze, and glazes.

Process

Once the pitcher reaches the bone dry stage, apply the terra sigillata. To decorate similarly to the pitcher shown here, start by drawing a vertical line in pencil that divides the piece in half. Using a wide, soft bristled brush, apply the terra sigillata so it covers the entire piece with the exception of a narrow band under the pencil line (figure 1). Before putting the pitcher aside, brush on a second layer of terra sigillata. After the first two layers of terra sig have dried for several hours to overnight, brush on a third layer.

Bisque the piece then brush a thin layer of oxide wash over the entire piece. Next, wipe the majority of the oxide away with a damp sponge, leaving it only in the recessed texture to create a patina (figure 2). Wring your sponge out with fresh water often as you work. Note: Wear gloves and a dust mask when applying and removing oxide wash.

Next, apply a perimeter of auto pinstriping tape around the areas where you would like to add color. Brush on the appropriate thickness of underglaze or glaze within that perimeter (figure 3). In the case

Blunt-nosed pitcher, 10 inches (25 cm) in height, thrown and altered earthenware, terra sigillata and glaze, fired to cone 03. *Photo: Charlie Cummings.*

of this pitcher, I use two layers each of red underglaze and Rick Hirsch Matte Robin's Egg glaze. The final step of the exterior decoration is to cover the glazed area with wax resist (leave the underglaze line unwaxed). Use the point of a needle tool to release and remove the tape from your bisqueware. Generally the tape leaves a nice clean edge.

When the wax is dry, pour your favorite liner glaze inside, carefully cover the interior, and pour the glaze out. Allow enough time for the piece to dry again before dipping the exterior into a transparent glaze.

Creating Layers and Depth

1. Applying terra sigillata to the bone-dry pitcher.

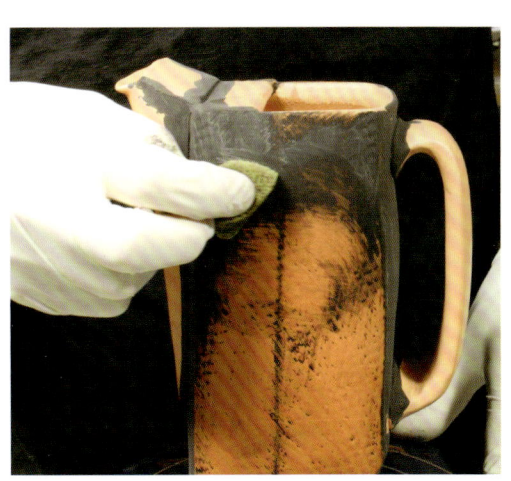

2. Wiping away excess oxide patina from the bisque-fired pitcher.

3. Applying underglaze in areas masked off with auto-pinstriping tape resist.

PINNELL/BRICKELL TERRA SIGILLATA BASE

Water	2 parts
Clay	1 part
Sodium silicate	0.5%

Mix clay and water together and blunge with a drill mixer for 5–10 minutes. Add the sodium silicate and mix for another 5 minutes. Place the container on a table and leave undisturbed for 6–8 hours. Siphon center layer into another container. This is the terra sigillata.

WHITE SIGILLATA BASE

Water	20 lb
XX Saggar Clay	10 lb
Sodium Silicate	22.7 grams

Mix, allow to settle then siphon per Terra Sig Base. For opaque white, add 1 tablespoon of titanium dioxide to 1 cup of white sigillata. For adobe pink, add 2 tablespoons of yellow ochre to 1 cup of white sigillata.

RED SIGILLATA BASE

Water	20 lb
Red Art Clay	10 lb
Sodium Silicate	22.7 grams

Mix, allow to settle then siphon per Terra Sig Base.

KENDALL BLACK STAIN

Gerstley Borate	48%
Ferro Frit 3124	12
Black Iron Oxide	24
Black Copper Oxide	16
Cobalt Oxide	pinch
	100%

VC 5000 SATIN TRANSPARENT CONE 04

Whiting	7%
Ferro Frit 3124	77
F-4 Feldspar (Minspar 200)	14
EPK Kaolin	2
	100%

RICK HIRSCH SATIN MATTE BASE
Cone 03–04

Gerstley Borate	32.0%
Lithium Carbonate	8.9
Whiting	16.7
Nepheline Syenite	3.9
EPK Kaolin	3.9
Silica	34.6
	100.0%
Add: Bentonite	2.0%

Robin's Egg

Add: Rutile	4.0%
Copper Carbonate	2.0%

Creating Layers and Depth
WATERCOLOR MAIOLICA

by Laurie Curtis

Maiolica is described in Wikipedia as "Italian tin-glazed pottery dating from the Renaissance. It's decorated in bright colors on a white background, frequently depicting historical and legendary scenes. The name is thought to have come from the medieval Italian word for Majorca, an island on the route for ships bringing Hispano-Moresque wares from Valencia to Italy, although the tin-glazed ware originated in Iraq (then Mesopotamia) in an attempt to replicate white Tang Chinese ware. Modern day maiolica is now painted in many different styles throughout the world but the materials and method basically remain the same (although we can no longer use lead in our colors and Zircopax often replaces the expensive tin oxide as the primary opacifier in many maiolica glaze recipes).

Watercolor Techniques

While the basic materials remain the same, different painting styles can be adapted to maiolica to achieve unique results. Ceramic stains and underglazes mixed with water painted on unfired white-glazed bisque is very much the same as painting a watercolor painting on paper. Both techniques require that you use soft brushes, mix pigment/stain with water and apply them to an absorbent surface. While painting on top of glaze, your colors will absorb instantly and stay where you have dropped the brush stroke. While painting on paper, your watery colors will be absorbed more slowly and can move around or travel before they settle (figure 1). Sometimes (unintentionally or intentionally) colors will bleed into other colors and create magic. There is a different kind of magic that results in painting on top of an unfired glazed piece of pottery. The joy of opening your kiln and seeing a beautiful painting technique that only high heat and atmospheric conditions could have created.

Getting Started

To create my watercolor maiolica, I start with a handbuilt piece of terra-cotta bisque (fired to cone 04) and brush on two or three layers of white glaze. I prefer to use a commercially made

Creating Layers and Depth

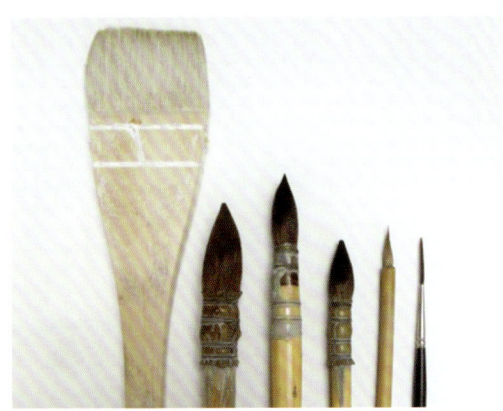

The brushes I like to use (from top to bottom): A synthetic-hair, fine liner brush; very soft natural hair round quill brushes; and a white goat-hair, flat wash brush.

Colors for maiolica watercolor painting. Hobby Colorobbia Bisque Strokes underglaze, Mason stains, and manganese dioxide.

1. Colors flow and bleed in this painting of satsuma oranges on paper. This effect doesn't happen with watercolor maiolica.

2. Mix Mason stains on white plates. Group blues and reds to make shades of purples, and group yellows with blues and greens.

white dipping glaze from Italy (Hobby Colorobbia) and have experimented making my own but find I always go back to the Italian glaze. I use it both for dipping small pieces and brushing or pouring it on the larger pieces. After I've completely covered my piece in white glaze I let it dry completely overnight. Wearing a dust mask, I always lightly hand sand my pieces over a water-filled sink to remove any bumps and create a smooth base for painting. There will always be more glaze dust created while you sand but either leave it on the surface of the piece (it will dissolve when you apply the watercolors) or tap it off but don't blow on it as the materials are harmful to breathe in. Sometimes I start painting my piece by brushing on a lightly colored wash, which is basically a mixture of stains and lots and lots of water. I try to avoid going over an area with my wide soft brush more than once. I let the piece dry again overnight. It's very important to work on a very dry glaze surface.

I then take the piece and improvise a design in my mind by thinking of a specific fruit and start drawing it lightly with a dull pencil directly on top of the dried white glaze. If the composition isn't quite right, I lightly rub out the pencil lines and redraw it. Never use an eraser because it has oil in it that will repel the colorants. I tend to always keep in mind the five basic design elements color, line, shape, texture, and mass or size rela-

3. After applying a wash, fill in the light yellow of the lemon within the pencil lines that define the image, working from light to dark.

4. Once the basic shapes of the fruit are defined, it's time to mix colors for the darker elements like leaves and stems.

5. Start painting the leaves, mixing stain colors on the plate and double loading the brush with greens and yellows.

6. Finish painting the leaves, adding darker shading to the outside edges by double loading darker greens and blues.

tionships when creating a design. I also always try to paint an odd number of main objects like three oranges as opposed to two or four oranges. One orange will work visually, but it should be placed slightly off center with leaves to balance it. I usually start with the main fruit and fill in the spaces with different sizes of leaves or blossoms. After I'm happy with the composition, I start painting.

Mixing Colors

I usually fill up two or three palettes with different colors (all Mason stain, Italian underglaze, and water mixtures), one with greens and yellow and the others with orange, red, and yellow or blues and reds to make purple. I use white plates for mixing my washes and little separate bowls for brown, pink, manganese, and dark blue (figure 2). I then fill my round, natural-hair quill brush with the watered down stain/underglaze mixtures (no added frit), working from light to dark to create a transparent layered look (figures 3–8).

The amount of stain and underglaze mixed with water varies based on the intensity desired. Start with around 1 part stain/underglaze mixture to 20 parts water. I create the colors by sight and feel. The more water you use, the lighter and more transparent the color will be. You can tell you need to add more water if your brush starts to skip or drag across the surface of your piece. Your brush stroke should glide across the top of the unfired white glaze.

Creating Layers and Depth

7. Shade one edge of the lemon with light green to create a sense of depth and roundness.

8. Shade the opposite side of each lemon to create depth, then add a little blue wash to the bottoms for a darker shadow.

9. Mix manganese dioxide with water to create a wash, then outline everything using a fine liner brush.

Brushing Techniques

Learning the best speed and pressure of your brush stroke is important. There are many Chinese brush-stroke books available with great exercises that are helpful, and I recommend *Chinese Brush Painting* by Pauline Cherrett and *The Art of Chinese Brush Painting* by Lucy Wang.

After I have painted all the colors of the design and have added shading and accents like sun spots for depth, brown for the stems, and blue hues for shadows on the bottom of the lemons, I'm ready to add outlines. I follow the traditional Italian maiolica technique of outlining everything with a manganese dioxide wash (figure 9). Some artists use black Mason stain, but I love the grainy texture and softer color of manganese. I use a very fine liner brush, dipping it often into water first, then into the manganese and water wash when creating the lines. As I load the brush, I'm constantly stirring the colorant up in the bowl of wash because manganese dioxide doesn't stay mixed with water. I like that quality about it because it fires looking slightly grainy. Once outlines are finished, I paint the back and the rim of the piece (figure 10).

Handling and Firing

I carry pieces to the electric kiln using my fingertips, usually holding onto an edge where the glaze has worn off during the painting process and the clay is showing along the rim. I don't usually touch up that edge because it adds to the character of the piece, but you can do this once its in the kiln. I then fire my pieces to cone 06 (figure 11).

Troubleshooting & Experimenting

Watercolor painting on an unfired glazed surface isn't always easy. Over time I've learned the power of improvisation by transforming a mistake, drip, or a smudge into an extra leaf, flower, or stem rather than trying to remove it. You can't brush over one area more than once or twice without picking up the white glaze underneath, especially when using so much water. This muddies the color and takes away from the transparent quality of the painting. No matter how hard

10. Touch up anything that needs extra color, paint a wash on the bottom, add your signature and date, and paint the rim.

11. Before firing, the painting is softer (center bowl). After firing, the colors are brighter and lines blend in more (bowl on the left).

the limitations seem when you're learning the process, you'll be rewarded when you open the kiln and see the beautiful luminosity of layered, transparent colors sealed in glaze.

I have been painting watercolor maiolica for many years now. It came together after studying fabric design, traditional watercolor painting and drawing, Chinese brush painting, and basic ceramic handbuilding techniques using slabs and molds. None of these practices would have come together if it weren't for an Italian friend introducing me to Italian maiolica ceramic products. I fell in love with the materials and the process instantly and spent many hours exploring the different personalities of each color (mostly made from mineral oxides) and how easily they could be mixed and applied like traditional watercolors. There were many trials and errors but eventually I came to know which ones needed more dilution etc. Eventually, I decided to add Mason stains to the colorful liquid underglazes I was using. The stains are less expensive and can be bought locally in loose bulk. So I now use a mixture of liquid underglaze colors along with the Mason stains using them alone or mixed together on my palette. Sometimes using analogous colors on my palette, I double and triple load my brush to create more interesting brush strokes. Along with omitting the frit, I realized I didn't have to follow the traditional method of maiolica painting by finishing my piece with a layer of clear glaze. My tested watercolor palette was diluted enough to allow the base white glaze to absorb it all and seal it into a smooth gloss finish.

Inspiration and Sources

The inspiration for all my shapes and designs comes from my long-time obsession with vintage pottery and fabric design mostly decorated with beautiful common fruits and flowers. A weekly visit to my local Farmer's Market also inspires me. I especially love looking at all the colors on the apricots, plums, peaches, and the different kinds of apples. While driving I make an effort to stop when I come upon an orchard or a vineyard and check out how the fruit, blossoms, and leaves are attached to the branches. I don't try to replicate them exactly but it helps to have some mental reference. After years of selling pottery I have discovered that people are more likely to buy a piece if they recognize and can name the fruit or flowers they see in my designs.

Creating Layers and Depth
STAINS, SLIPS AND PATIENCE

by Scott Ziegler

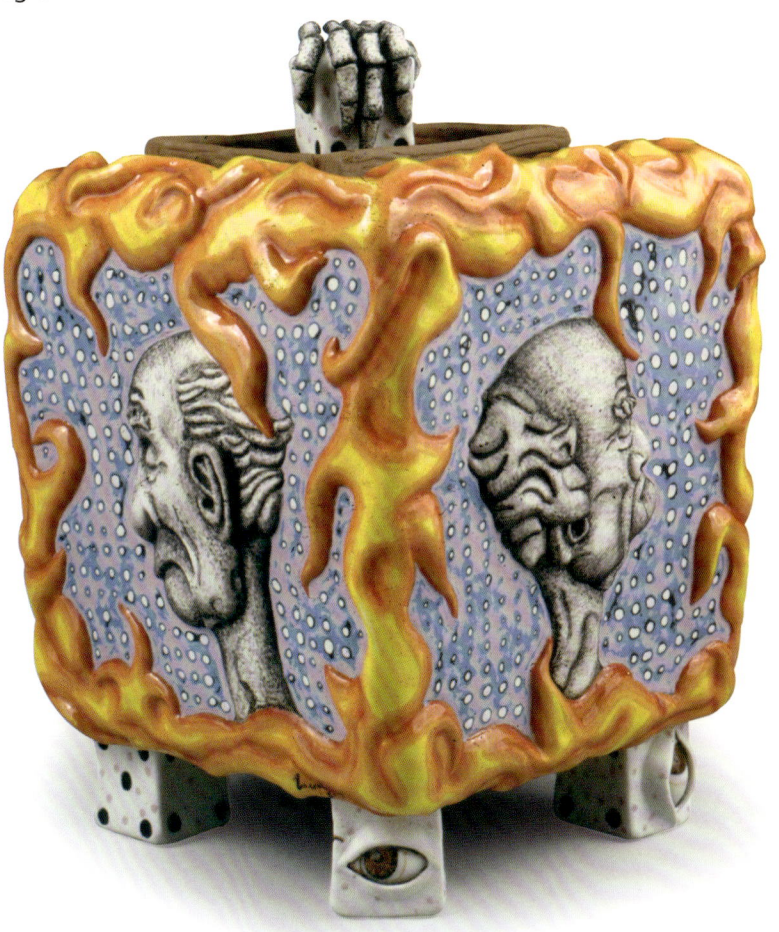

Roll Model, 7 inches (18 cm) in height, colored slips and glazes, fired to cone 6. *Photos by Jeffrey Dionesotes*

When my work is bone dry, I use a variety of grades of sandpaper to smooth out imperfections. After it is completely smooth, I begin to lay in my color. I create my own colored slips by adding different percentages of commercial stains to the same porcelain clay body used for my pieces, adding water until they become quite fluid. It's generally not wise to add wet clay to bone-dry clay, because it will crack off, but since the clay in the slip is really just an agent for binding color onto the surface, I can get away with applying many thin layers. That is the trick, but the process is very time consuming. Each area requires three to four brush coats per color. When all the color has been applied, I'm finally able to bisque fire the piece. For the glaze firing, I add glossy and matt glaze and fire to cone 6.

Glazing Techniques

Expiration Date, 13 inches (33 cm) in length, porcelain, colored slips and glazes, fired to cone 6. Photo courtesy of the artist.

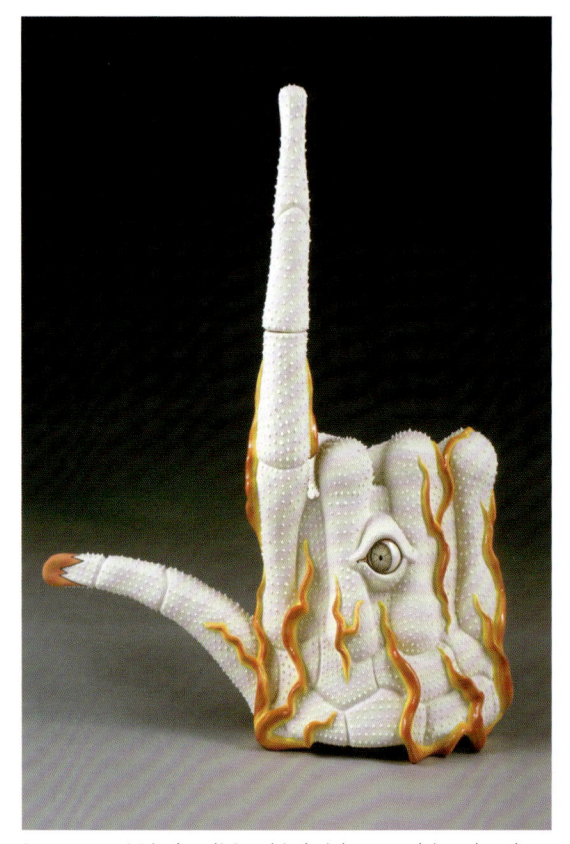

Innocence, 14 inches (36 cm) in height, porcelain colored slips and glazes, fired to cone 6.

The Adversary, 9 inches (23 cm) in height, porcelain, colored slips and glazes, fired to cone 6.

Creating Layers and Depth
ADDING DEPTH TO YOUR GLAZES

by Lisa Bare Culp

As a potter and in-home instructor for many years, I've always mixed my own glazes, or relied on other professionals who mix dry glazes to my specifications. Recently, an idea for a single pot challenged me to experiment with commercially-made glazes. The outcome has been succesful with vibrant new color selections, time savings and the convenience of readily available glazes screened for toxicity—all this without compromising my workspace or my standards.

What changed my thinking on commercially prepared glazes was my desire to introduce bold new colors into my work. I envisioned a piece with contrasting matt black-and-white slip surfaces offset against a single area glazed in vibrant red. My local supplier recommended a food-safe, non-toxic red glaze, Mayco's Stroke & Coat Cone 06.

Early tests resulted in pieces with dramatic and beautiful contrasts between my porcelain slips and the red glaze. In one test, I used Stroke & Coat SC-73 Candy Apple Red, to highlight areas of bisqueware. In another, I used SC-74 Hot Tamale. Sometimes I applied the glaze with a big brush in a single, expressive stroke. Other times, I squeezed the colors from a slip trailer and a turkey baster.

After these loose applications, I dipped the entire piece in my usual cone 6 glazes. Because

Fish Bowl, matt white glaze over commercial glazes, fired to cone 6.

of their gum content, the commercial glazes resisted my glazes slightly, making the bold strokes of color come through vividly. Stroke edges were blended and their colors softly striking against the cone 6 palette. The outcome was as satisfying technically as it was aesthetically; I was satisfied with the melt (Stroke & Coat is a glaze, not an underglaze), the color and the absence of pinholing or other major flaws at cone 6.

A New Tool

Further experiments with sgraffito, layering, mixing with slip and stoneware glazes, and multiple firings have opened up commercial glazes as a new artistic tool—albeit an unexpected one—to share with students. They have learned the importance

Glazing Techniques

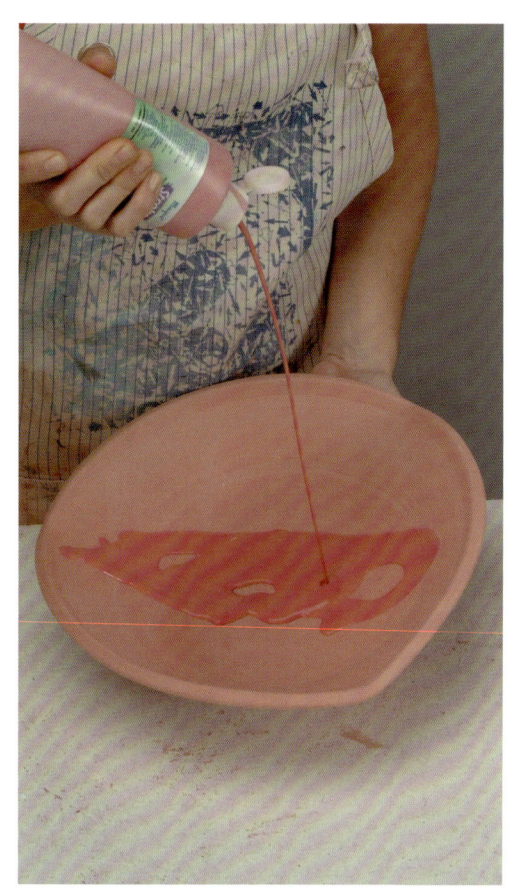

1. Squeeze a large amount of Stroke & Coat SC-73 Candy Apple Red on the interior of a bisque-fired bowl.

2. Apply a thick coat of glazes with a large brush to the interior surface of a leather-hard bowl.

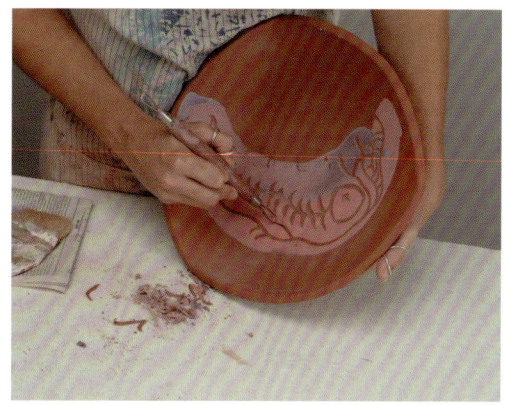

3. Once the colors are slightly dry, the design is carved through the glaze with a loop tool.

of experimenting with new surfaces, new materials, combining techniques and achieving balance with different kinds of material.

If you'd like to experiment with commercially prepared glazes, I've included three of my projects for you to try. Mixing my own recipes will always be an important part of understanding the science behind the art of pottery making. But successfully integrating commercial glazes in the mix is just one more way to pursue the function and beauty of ceramics.

Pouring

Squeeze a large amount of Stroke & Coat SC-73 Candy Apple Red across the interior of a bisque-fired bowl (figure 1). Use a 2-inch brush to apply a thin coat of Mayco's Elements Chunkies EL 203 Coal Dust (this is a low-fire effect glaze with crystals) over the Candy Apple Red. A nice feathered edge is created when the piece is dipped into a cone 6 black glossy glaze (figure 2).

Carving

Apply a thick coat of Mayco Stroke & Coat SC-71 Purple-Licious and SC-74 Hot Tamale with a large brush to the interior surface of a leather-hard bowl (figure 3). Once the colors are slightly dry, the design is carved through the glaze with a loop tool (figure 4), then bisque fired to cone 08. Dip the entire piece twice in a cone 6 matt white glaze and fire to cone 6 in oxidation. The commercial colors show well through the white matt. Note: If the carved lines are too fine they may fill in when the glaze melts.

Creating Layers and Depth

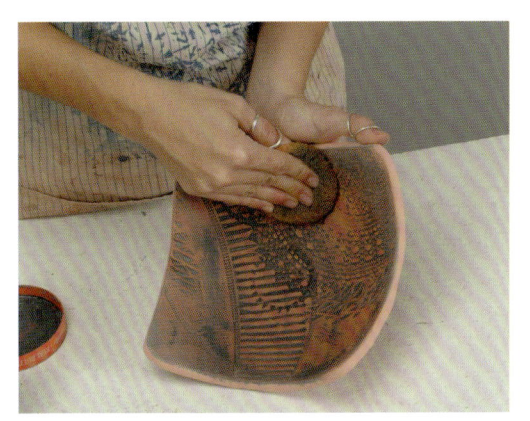

5. Apply a cone 6 porcelain black slip as a stain, wiping off the high spots with a damp sponge.

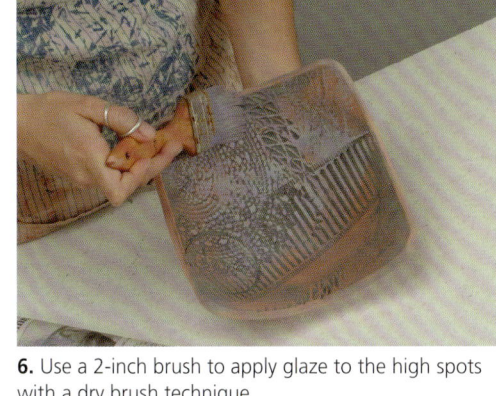

6. Use a 2-inch brush to apply glaze to the high spots with a dry brush technique.

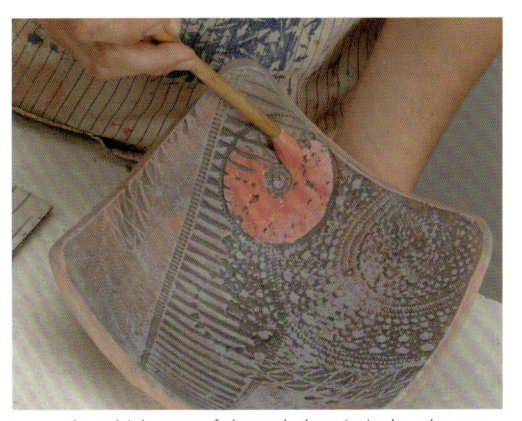

7. Apply a thick coat of the red glaze in isolated areas to obtain a bright color.

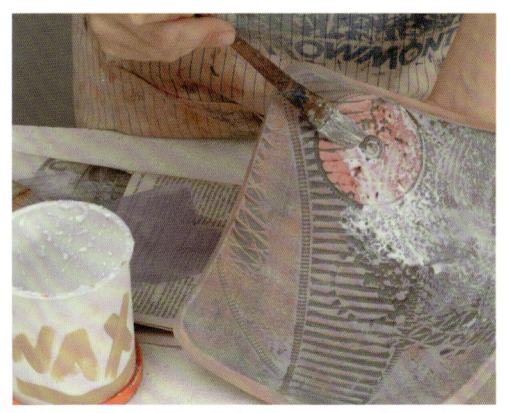

8. Apply wax resist to the interior surface of the piece.

Layering

On a heavily textured, bisque-fired piece, apply a cone 6 porcelain black slip as a stain, wiping off the high spots with a damp sponge (figure 5). Use a 2-inch brush to apply Stroke & Coat SC-71 Purple-Licious to the high spots with a dry brush technique (figure 6). Next, dry brush Mayco's Stroke & Coat Red SC-74 Hot Tamale and SC-27 Sour Apple onto the interior. Apply a thick coat of the red glaze in isolated areas to obtain a bright color (figure 7). Apply wax resist to the interior surface of the piece (figure 8) and allow to dry. Dip the entire piece in a cone 6 blue glaze.

Fired dish showing results of layering.

Creating Layers and Depth
TEXTILE INSPIRED DESIGNS

by Colleen Riley

Bowl, 8 inches (20 cm) in diameter, light-colored stoneware, matte green glaze, soda fired.

I grew up surrounded by textiles. My mother was an accomplished seamstress, performing a small miracle on every homecoming and prom dress she made for her four daughters. We spent many delightful hours together at the fabric store, in collaborative exploration of every possibility for an upcoming outfit. My grandmother, who lived nearby, always had a quilt, embroidery, or crochet project in the works. My father was stationed in India during World War II. He brought back artifacts that were profoundly exotic to a girl from the Midwest, such as a carved wooden cigarette box and an ivory-inlaid cribbage board. My favorite artifact was a piece of sari cloth woven with silver thread. Sadly, that cloth was destroyed in a flood many years ago, but it remains indelibly etched in my memory.

I admire the luscious bare clay surfaces produced in our soda kiln. But I'm also drawn to the rich, reactive surfaces of saturated matte glazes. In an effort to bring both into my work, I've refined a technique that exploits the best qualities of bare clay and

Creating Layers and Depth

1. Apply slip to a leather-hard form. Experiment with different brushes to create raised textures (cheap hardware store brushes work well).

2. Once slip has dried a bit and is no longer shiny, use the edge of a rasp to scratch texture through the slip and onto the pot.

3. Sketch a design on the bisqued piece with a pencil then brush on wax over the scratched texture, filling in the design.

4. Pour glaze over the slipped, carved, and waxed layers to create an additional final color layer.

glazed matte surfaces in a soda firing, while referencing the textures and patterns found in textiles.

Process

I start by applying slip to the leather-hard form (figure 1). This is not a traditional thin flashing slip for soda firing, it's made from my clay body, with added colorants such as iron and black stain, and mixed to a heavy cream consistency. Any favorite slip or engobe is worth a try, with or without colorants. After the slip has dried a bit, I scratch through the slip to create a texture or rough pattern (figure 2). This creates the impression of threads in a tapestry. I resist the tendency to over-design this bottom layer, considering that this texture will fight with the overlaying design if they are both too busy. (Always wear a dust mask when scratching or carving dry clay.)

After bisque firing, I add another design by brushing with wax resist, envisioning a subtractive effect similar to batik (figure 3). After the wax dries, I pour or dip the final glaze layer (figure 4). To avoid opaque, dense-looking surfaces, my glazes are generally applied thinner than they would be for

93

Glazing Techniques

traditional stoneware firing. This allows the underlying colored slip and texture to bleed through, often creating a third different color.

Since this surface can be complex, the interior of a bowl is glazed simply (figure 5). To create a subtle, ghosted effect I may add a complementary design of the exterior in a slightly contrasting glaze underneath the liner glaze. Or, apply wax resist in a simple pattern near the rim of the glaze, keeping in mind that the soda is likely to affect bare clay only near the rim of the interior.

This two-step decorating process allows me to tap into my inner textile-designer self, giving great flexibility to explore patterns in a broad palette of slip/glaze effects. It's taken a lot of experimentation to narrow down the most successful combinations, and every firing reveals yet more possibilities. The soda acts as a wash, softening the transition areas between bare clay, slip, and glaze, pulling the elements together into a more cohesive whole.

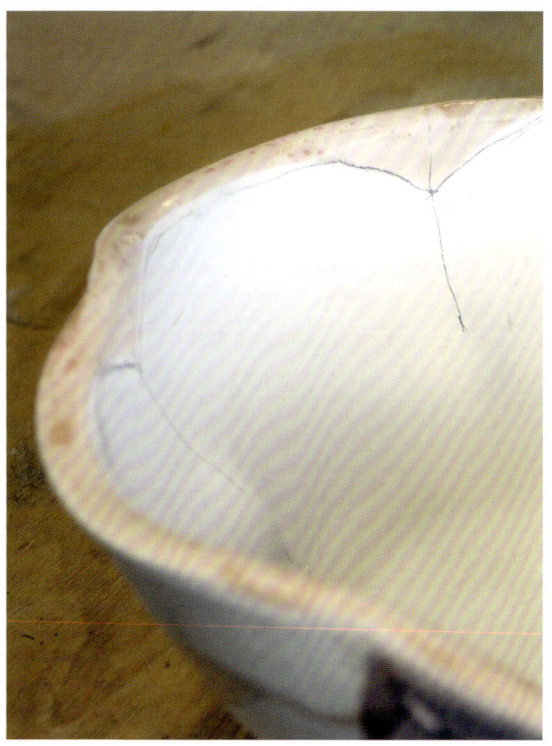

5. Before glazing, apply an interior wax pattern near the rim. Leaving some clay exposed adds soda effects to the inside.

6. Several bowls with finished layered surfaces ready for the glaze firing

Creating Layers and Depth

Bowl with squared rim and foot detail, 9 inches (23 cm) in diameter, light-colored stoneware, layered slip and glazes, soda fired.

Creating Layers and Depth
HUNT PROTHRO'S STAINS AND UNDERGLAZES

by Susan Chappelear

Platter, 20 inches in diameter, porcelain with underglazes, stains and Gerstley borate wash, fired to cone 6.

Hunt Prothro was introduced to pottery during the seventies through study with Marguerite Wildenhain at Pond Farm in Sonoma County, California. Prothro attests that the legacy of those summer workshops is a continuing presence in his life and in his work. Wildenhain was influential in mid-century ceramics and is widely regarded for the integrity of craftsmanship applied to utilitarian vessels.

Using porcelain, he throws platters, bowls and cylinders in preparation for a cone 10 reduction firing with light reduction. Referring to early Greek pottery, Prothro prefers vessels with thick rims and shapes echoing the human figure. As a metaphor for the human longing for touch, his bowls invite handling.

His admiration for the American abstract painter Arshille Gorky is evidenced by the painterly passages of color and lyrical line. As in Gorky's canvases, the platters are intriguing, with spatial ambiguity marked by ethereal line. Chiaroscuro, which appears in the bowls as sharply defined, adjacent elliptical shapes of light and dark, is, however, more atmospheric in the platters. Accents of hard-edged shapes provide a focal point as they appear suspended in infinity. An oriental landscape can be imagined, or for some the platters may trigger a reference to Western action painting.

Creating Layers and Depth

Prothro brushes stains into incised textures before carefully wiping off the excess.

Complementary colors are sponged on to enliven the surface.

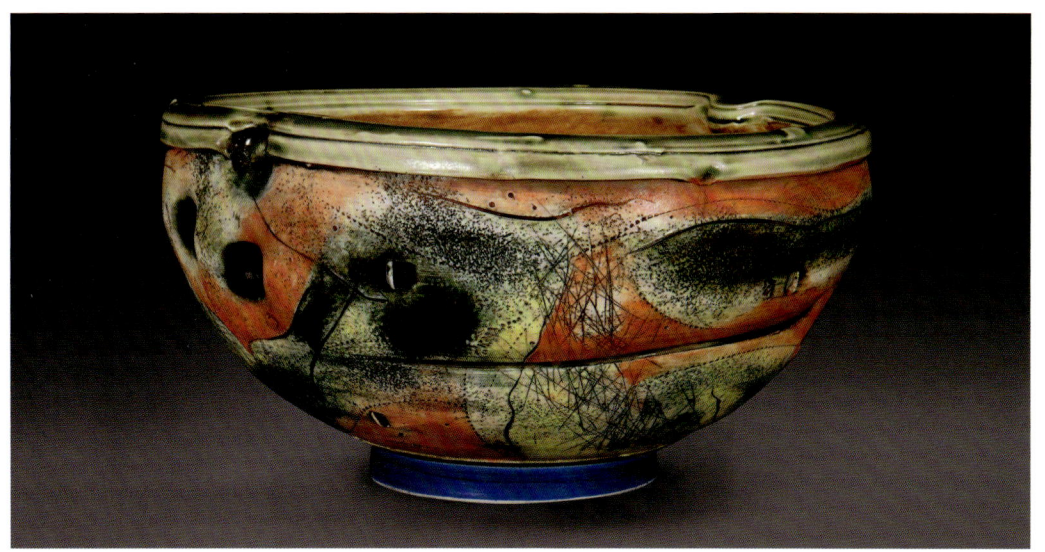

Blue Dot Bowl, 14 inches in diameter, porcelain with underglazes and stains, fired to cone 10.

Mixing It Up

Although Prothro's underglazes are poured on a palette, he achieves all of the color mixing on the bisqued pot itself. He follows a sequence to keep all surfaces clean. He applies color to the foot, then the interior and the exterior. The inside of the bowls are often painted in counterpoint to the exterior; related, but distinct. He says, "The rim is a third area, a point of transition, and a zone of change with all the attendant hesitations and gestures of finality."

He applies broad strokes of black stain to all sgraffittoed surfaces, then gently wipes, leaving only the inlay to provide sharp contrast to the warm underglazes to follow. Without any masking, he carefully paints and dabs each piece to preserve a grid arrangement. In some of the pieces, figure and ground appear to be on the same plane, as hard-edged regions of color are juxtaposed to create contrasting tonal values and heighten each other's vital nature. This interplay of shapes and colors, which have no representational associations, take on a painterly quality. In other pieces, he achieves coloration by scumbling layers of translucent washes, some of which he spritzes with water to promote color bleeding and to suggest distant galaxies. He preserves the color effects with a thin, Gerstley borate-based clear glaze and strives to achieve a patina rather than a true glaze.

4

Specialized Techniques
LOW-FIRE ELECTRIC REDS

by David L. Gamble

Above: Plate, by David Gamble. Cross is glazed with red underglaze.

Left: Untitled, by Scott Bennett. Amaco LM series Coral glaze with wax and Black overspray. As the wax melts in the kiln, the black moves.

I'll start by explaining there are two different types of commercial red glazes that I normally use. One type is an extremely bright color and harder to achieve and the other is a newer tomato red color that is AP (Approved Product of the Arts and Creative Materials Institute) nontoxic and dinnerware safe. The latter is formulated with inclusion stains, which are continuing to be improved. The color is encased in zircon, which makes them safe to use even in the classroom.

The AP nontoxic reds are extremely stable and were used to create red velvet underglazes that can be fired from cone 05 to as high as cone 10—only salt seems to blush them out.

The success of underglazes has allowed the development of gloss and matt red glazes that have been formulated to work well at the low-fire cone 05 range and other glazes formulated for the cone 4–6 range. These are extremely reliable. Three brushed coats will usually be enough of an application and you get nice tomato color reds at both temperatures.

Bright reds are not dinnerware safe and are extremely sensitive to variations in firing conditions. There have been many times that an art teacher has asked me about the use of these types of red glazes. I understand the space and time challenges that teachers face, but you cannot put these glazes in with your normal glaze firings and expect good results. They are affected by how tight the load is stacked, other glazes (mostly copper greens), and temperature. If you're firing to cone 05, I can almost guarantee there will be problems. The glaze will most likely have variations from clear to gray to black, and if you're lucky, a spot or two of red. Note: Amaco glazes were used in the pieces shown here, however, many companies produce similar glazes.

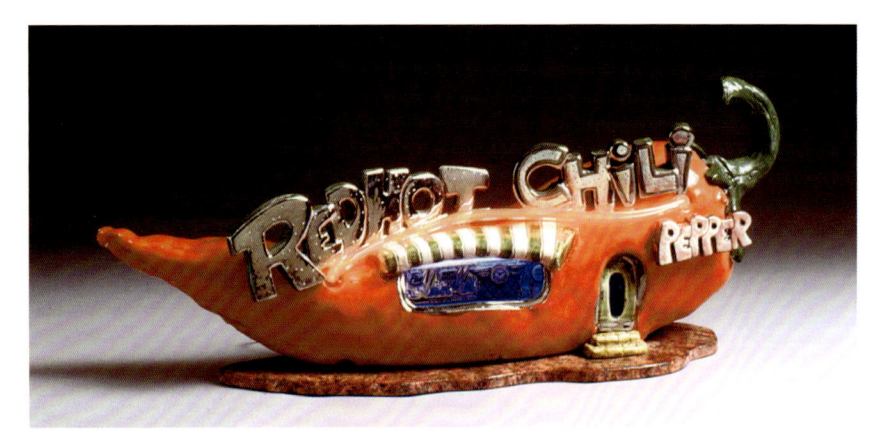

Redhot Chilli Pepper Diner, by Jerry Berta. Glazed with red underglazes.

Process

Here are my suggestions of what you need to know and do to achieve the bright reds.

- Bisque your clay body slowly to cone 04 (12 hours to get all the gases out). Although these glazes are not considered translucent, the clay body color does affect them slightly. White bodies will make the glaze appear brighter in color than darker bodies.
- Using a brush, apply the glaze thicker than the normal three coats. Four coats will usually work, but too heavy an application may cause the glaze to run. Glaze application may need experimentation and practice.
- Load the kiln very loosely. There is a need for lots of space between the pieces for air circulation. I leave the peephole plugs out during the firing, thus allowing extra oxygen to enter the kiln chamber.
- Do not fire above cone 06 (1828°F), preferably using witness cones for observation. I have been firing at cone 07 (1789°F) with great results. These glazes seem to like the cooler temperatures.
- Fire as quickly as you can, four hours is ideal. If your pieces are larger, an example being my 22-inch platters, take them up slowly to about 1200°F. This may help to eliminate cracking problems. Then turn the kiln on high to fast fire to the end of the firing.

Observations

If your kiln is vented through the bottom with a system that draws air through the top of the kiln, this will help give you more oxygen in the kiln and better red results. Remember that kilns, depending on how they are stacked, may not fire that evenly. This can cause cold spots and hot spots. There can be a difference in temperature equal to a couple of cones from top to bottom—depending where the kiln sitter or thermocouple is located. This variability can really affect bright red glazes. Newer kilns with zone control and multiple thermocouples tend to fire more evenly. If you have an older kiln, place cones in the top, middle and bottom of the kiln so you can keep a record of what happens in the firing. They can help provide answers if problems do occur.

I've been placing red glazes on different color clay bodies, layering over glazed fired pieces and layering one coat of gold glaze over the top.

I then place the pieces next to peep holes to brighten the color, or place shelves over the edges to deepen and take away the color. This is what is exciting to me—not getting it perfect, but having the surface color change and vary while having some control over what the changes will be. I am an avid advocate of using commercial glazes the way a painter would use his tubes of paint. Experiment, test to the "max" and make them your own. Don't be afraid to experiment.

Specialized Techniques

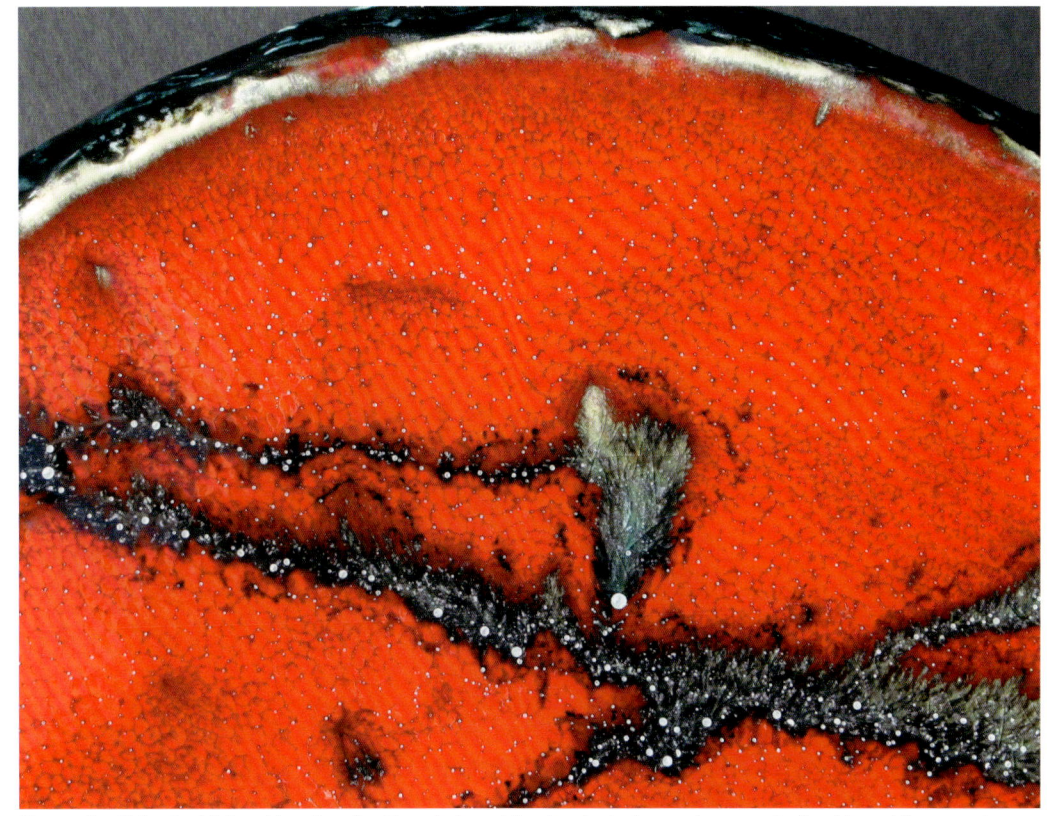

Platter detail, by David Gamble, glazed with red glaze, blue brush strokes and one coat of gold used for accents.

Platter, by David Gamble, glazed with red glaze and blue brush strokes on top.

Specialized Techniques
MASTERING MICA

by Kate and Will Jacobson

For the past year, we've been exploring the subtle luster and compelling color palette of mica as a glaze element. We usually teach naked raku, but wanted to give our students some other low-fire techniques to explore. While preparing for a workshop, we tested the reaction of various terra sigillatas, colored porcelain slips, and even acrylic paint in the ferric chloride saggar process.

Why did we try a copper-colored acrylic paint? We discovered the pigment in the copper color is mica coated with titanium and iron. We thought it would be a good source for these oxides. Turns out, it was a good source of mica.

Mica, a mineral often used in cosmetics for it shimmery essence and in electronics for its insulating properties, is a very refractory mineral. It easily withstands the 1472°F (800°C), (cone 015), temperature a lot of bare-clay firing techniques call for, making it ideal for using in several low-fire techniques such as naked raku, ferric chloride saggar, horsehair firing, clay saggar and pit-fired ceramics. Detailed explanations of these firing techniques are well covered in the book *Naked Raku and Related Bare Clay Techniques* published by The American Ceramic Society (www.CeramicArtsDaily.org/bookstore).

Glazing with Mica

There are several ways to use mica as a glaze element in low-fire techniques. Wearing a dusk mask, mix 5 grams of mica powder into one cup of terra sigillata made from OM4 ball clay.

Life Aquatic, sponged and painted with copper colored "mica paint" and block printed on the surface, ferric-chloride fired.

This will give you a starting point for your color. The more mica you add, the more saturated the color becomes.

Next, brush two coats of plain terra sigillata on a bone dry piece. Then apply a topcoat of the mica sigillata. This can be brushed, sponged, painted, stamped, sprayed, etc. (figures 1 and 2).

Specialized Techniques

1. Applying mica paint (matte acrylic medium mixed with ½ gram of colored mica powder) with a stamp.

2. Brushing a top coat of Jacobson's Super Copper mica sigillata on top of 2 coats of regular OM4 sigillata.

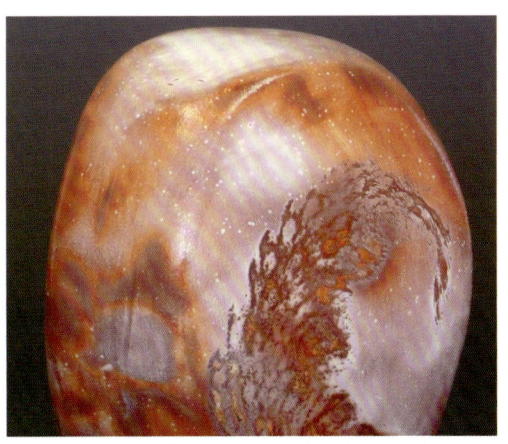

3. *Wave*, OM4 sigillata, copper-colored mica paint sponged on surface, ferric chloride fired.

4. Applying colored mica dry rub onto a slightly dry, textured clay surface with a soft bristle make-up brush.

When dry, burnish with a piece of plastic wrap and bisque fire to 1382°F, (cone 017). Your piece is now ready to be used in one of many low-fire techniques. The mica gives an added luster and subtle sheen that emanates from within the clay. This application also works well with any bare clay technique that fire at or under 1472°F.

Making Mica Paint

Another way to use mica is to mix your own mica paint. This is particularly effective in ferric chloride, aluminum-foil saggar firings. Mix two tablespoons of matte acrylic medium (available at art supply stores) with ½ gram of colored mica powder. Paint or sponge this mixture onto an already bisque-fired pot that has been coated with either regular OM4 terra sigillata or mica sigillata.

Once dry, and wearing latex gloves and a respirator, paint or pour ferric chloride on the piece. Then, wrap the piece with two layers of aluminum foil, making sure you get a tight seal. Fire the piece rapidly to 1472°F, then back off the temperature to 1382°F and hold for 10 minutes. Warning: Wear an appropriate respirator when firing with ferric chloride as you must take extreme caution to not inhale the fumes.

After firing and unwrapping the piece, take a soft brush and remove some of the residual dust.

Glazing Techniques

5. *Pineapple,* 10 inches (25 cm) in height, Laguna Amador Clay, mica dry rub, heated and smoked.

In order to fix the surface, use a UV-resistant fixative spray to seal and protect (figure 3).

We have discovered that one of the properties of mica is that it does not trap carbon. This is good news because it allows for contrast between the clay and mica in a smoke firing. This technique works well with highly textured forms. We like to call this the 'dry rub' technique. Use a soft bristle make-up brush to scrub dry mica powder onto a not-quite-leather-hard pot (figure 4). The mica is pushed into the clay and then the excess is brushed off. Bisque fire the piece to cone 017. Now it's ready to fire in a raku kiln followed by reduction in a smoke chamber. The result is shimmering mica embedded into the clay juxtaposed against the matte black of the carbon-infused clay (figure 5).

Mica Sources

- www.TKBTrading.com: TKB Trading has hundreds of colors to choose from. We have tried about 50. The reds seem to change or fade. The greens hold up nicely. The blues change a little but hold up okay. The copper, gold, and the silver colors hold up the best. The ferric chloride saggar technique is the hardest on the mica and causes more fading and color change. The colors we recommend are Breath of Spring, Deep Blue, Pearl Green, Emerald, Pennsylvania Green, Swiss Chocolate, Patagonia Purple, Glitter Siena, and Gold Lamé.
- www.EarthPigment.com: From Earth Pigments, we recommend Super Copper and Sterling Silver.

Specialized Techniques
THE COLORFUL WORLD OF MAJOLICA

by Linda Arbuckle

The majolica technique is commonly done at low-fire temperatures, although you may work in a similar way on any stiff, opaque glaze at other temperatures with related results. Most of the stain colors used for majolica decorating will fire to mid range (cone 5–6). At cone 10, shino glazes are very viscous and don't move much, but the available palette of colors is different: many of the purples fire out blue; yellows in reduction are often pale and grayish; most of the pinks burn out; and body stains (e.g., Mason Stain 6020 Pink) may be too refractory even at cone 10. Nevertheless, it maybe worth an experiment or two.

Small Pour: Sunflowers with Black Band, 5 inches (13 cm) in length, terra cotta with majolica glazes, fired to cone 04.

History and Name

Majolica (or maiolica) in common contemporary parlance is a white, opaque, glossy glaze that is very viscous to the point that it doesn't move during firing. This allows line quality applied to the raw glaze to be maintained faithfully through the firing process.

Historically, Middle Eastern potters developed such glazes for use over an earthenware clay at low temperatures. They used tin oxide to make a white, opaque glaze (usually fluxed with lead) that was a good ground for colored decoration. Work from the Middle East made using this method is identified as tin-glazed earthenware. A raw glaze surface was decorated with copper (green), manganese (plum), and iron or antimony (amber/yellow) over a glaze. Cobalt blues were very popular for decoration, and the blue-on-white echoed Asian high-fire ceramics. Metallic reduced lusterware (done in an additional firing) was also developed in the Middle East, often on a tin glaze.

When the Muslims conquered northern Africa, came north across the Strait of Gibraltar, and created a Moorish influence in Spain from the early 8th century until 1492, they brought their pottery technologies and aesthetics with them. This included tin-glazed pottery methods. Spain exported these wares from Majorca, and Italians began calling this tin-glazed ware majolica.

There are contemporary disagreements about the spelling, pronunciation, and terminology of majolica vs. maiolica. I suspect that the origins of the differences reside in what happens when a Spanish J is transliterated into another language, and complicated by casual use of terms for things that are not technically related. For instance, in the 19th century, companies produced molded relief wares with bright, jewel-like, transparent, colored lead glazes. The Minton company in England was well known for the production of these wares (teapots in the shape of pineapples and cauliflower, cheese bells in the form of beehives, etc.). The bright low-fire color reminded people of Italian majolica-decorated pottery, and the term majolica was used for both, although they are not technically related. I have seen texts that claim that the Minton–style work is done with techniques similar to Della Robbia techniques, but my eyes tell me it's not so. The tin-glazed work is seen spelled either way. The Minton–style work is usually spelled with a J. Some revisionists insist this is the only way, but very reputable sources, such as the Metropolitan Museum, have spelled the tin-glaze with a J.

Opacifiers

The use of only tin as an opacifier is often modified in contemporary practice. Tin makes a lovely, buttery, very opaque, white glaze. It also increases surface tension in a glaze and may aggravate crawling problems where the glaze is thick (e.g., in corners). Tin in amounts of 5% or above will also cause a color reaction with small amounts of chrome that will cause the tin glaze to turn pink (chrome fuming). This can be delightful if anticipated, but is often not kind to your color plans as a surprise. Many of the green and teal stain colors and some black stains contain chrome, and some rutiles con-

Bowl: Fruits of Our Labor in a Time of Envy, 11 inches (28 cm) in diameter, terra cotta with majolica glazes, fired to cone 04, 2010.

tain small amounts of chrome impurities that can cause chrome-tin pinking in high-tin glazes. For the above reasons, as well as the expense of tin oxide, many artists today use a zirconium opacifier, or a combination of some tin (for denser whiteness) with some zirconium opacifier. This would keep the amount of tin low (say under 4%), yet allow good opacity. Zirconium is weaker than tin in strength, and the usual rule is 1.5% zirconium to replace 1% tin. If chrome-tin pink fuming is a problem, drop the tin a bit, and add that amount multiplied by 1.5 of zirconium opacifier.

Some artists say they enjoy a bit of the terra cotta showing through a translucent white majolica glaze. For me, it darkens the glaze color, damps color response a bit, and makes any thick-thin areas of glaze application more noticeable than a more opaque white. I have always preferred a very white opaque glaze.

Majolica Colorant Suggestions

- Gerstley borate production has been erratic, and the material is variable in quality. It pushes decorating colors toward pastel through very fine reticulation (break up) of the glaze surface, and although I used it when I began majolica, I now use frit as a flux (with bentonite added) or commercial majolica decorating colors.
- Colorants mixed with only frit settle quickly, have limited brushability, and are very powdery once dry, making wax resist over the color smudge easily. Some artists use this powdery quality to work the movable surface like pastels. The addition of bentonite or CMC gum to the frit and colorant mix aids brushing and hardens the dry surface.
- Bentonite doesn't mix easily with water, so be sure to mix dry bentonite, frit, and colorant first, then add water. Some people find an immersion blender handy. I mix small amounts and generally use a tiny whisk. If something is really lumpy, I will use a small test sieve (60 mesh) and screen the mixture.
- I use Ferro frit 3124. Others will work, with color reactions influenced by the specific chemistry of each frit.
- To aid brushability, you may add a small amount of glycerin (drug store item), or a few drops liquid CMC gum to the liquid mix. Too much glycerin or gum can make a very slippery color mix that moves well but doesn't apply color in an even thickness.
- Colors in studio-mixed oxides or stains and commercial majolica decorating colors will generally mix, but some information about ceramic materials helps. I recommend doing line blends of colors to learn more about mixing and relative strength.
- Copper melts easily, and will color strongly compared to yellow colors. A nice chartreuse may be four parts yellow by volume to one part mixed copper.
- With paint, yellow + blue = green. In ceramic colors, blue is made with cobalt, a very strong colorant, while yellow may be a stain made with praseodymium or vanadium, which are weaker colorants than cobalt. Equal amounts of mixed yellow and blue decorating colors may still be very blue, due to the strength of cobalt.

Application Suggestions

Both the best and worst thing about majolica glaze is that it doesn't move when you fire it. Having a decent base glaze coating goes a long way toward being happy with the final product. Additionally, large bumps and voids in the raw glaze will leave evidence of brush strokes on top of them and emphasize your glaze application issues.

Apply glaze in the thinnest coating that will give you opacity, and attempt an even glaze coat. Dampen pieces slightly before dipping to remove any dust and moisten the ware for better glaze pick up. Dipping is my mode of choice, although I do know potters who spray effectively. I want to have a container that will allow me to do one dip of the bisqueware. If I have a piece that will not fit in my glaze bucket, say a long, oval platter, I use a different container for dipping. Garden stores often carry metal or plastic 5-gallon oval tubs. Oil change pans can be useful. I have flexible plastic tubs from a garden store that are wider than my 5-gallon glaze buckets, and will allow me to flex the bucket for longer-than-wide shapes and to form a spout to pour my glaze back into the bucket. In a pinch, I have used cardboard boxes reinforced with duct tape or dresser drawers double-lined with heavy trash bags to hold glaze for dipping.

For errors in glazing (and there are bound to be some) 400-grit wet-dry sandpaper will sand down lumps, or they may be gently scraped down with a sharp knife. When sanding or shaving glaze, do it over a container of water to trap the dust and prevent it from circulating in your studio environment.

Clay Body, Off-Gassing, Firing Rates

I am still experimenting with firing rates. Several years ago something in clay materials changed and caused gassing in my clay, resulting in many white gas dots in the fired majolica surface, where the base glaze might seal over, but the colorant layer is so thin that it can't seal and leaves a white spot. Many people maintain that firing slowly is the way to go, and it seems logical that any gas release would be more gentle the slower the firing. On the other hand, I fire many pieces in a small, oval, doll-body test kiln, which cools quickly, and these generally turn out less dotted. The same shapes fired about 200°F per hour in my regular kiln may be more dotted. It's been an infuriating problem that I continue to research. If you have dotting, try bisque firing as high as you can without making the work too dense to accept glaze. This may drive off gassy materials before glaze application and firing. Bisque at a slower rate, vent your kiln, and glaze thinner if possible. Thinner glaze is less likely to trap the gas bubbles and cause dotting.

Advantages

- The viscous glaze does not move when fired. The brushwork stays crisp, with no runny glaze to chip off shelves. Dry-footed areas need less margin on pot bottoms or lid seats.
- Because the raw glaze absorbs the color from the brush readily and does not move in the firing, the direction of brush marks, speed of the brush, and loading of the brush show in the fired decoration, adding painterly, expressive qualities to the marks.
- Thick glaze blankets the piece, which may forgive small handling errors like finger smudges in the surface.
- The kiln is a passive tool, resulting in more predictable results from firing to firing. Someone else could fire your work and achieve the same results (easier to share kilns).
- A bright palette of commercial stains gives easy access to a range of pinks, oranges, yellows, and purples that work well with the blue, green, and rust that are available with oxides.
- Inexpensive color, because it takes less colorant to put a thin wash on the glaze surface than to color a slip or a glaze.

Disadvantages

- The viscous glaze does not move when fired, which means any lumps, drips, or pinholes from application remain and do not heal over or smooth out in firing. Thick glaze may crawl.
- Because the raw glaze absorbs the color from the brush readily and does not move in firing, direction of brush marks, speed of the brush, and loading of the brush show in the fired decoration, and may reveal hesitancies, touch-ups, and direction of background when painting around motifs, etc., which may distract from the aesthetic impact.
- Thick glaze blankets the piece, which may cover small details in clay handling. like carving or incised decoration.
- The kiln is a passive tool, resulting in uniform color that may look flat or does not describe the form. There are no gifts from the kiln gods.
- The bright color may look garish, or the entire palette may look too pastel and therefore lose impact.

Specialized Techniques

ARBUCKLE MAJOLICA BASE GLAZE
Cone 03

Ferro Frit 3124	65.8 %
F-4 Feldspar (sub Minspar 200)	17.2
Nepheline Syenite	6.2
EPK Kaolin	10.8
	100.0 %
Add: Tin Oxide	4.0 %
Zircopax	9.0 %
Bentonite	2.0 %

ARBUCKLE MAJOLICA BASE GLAZE 2
Cone 05

Ferro Frit 3124	66.6 %
F-4 Feldspar (sub Minspar 200)	23.0
Nepheline Syenite	8.1
EPK Kaolin	2.3
	100.0 %
Add: Tin Oxide	4.0 %
Zircopax	9.0 %
Bentonite	2.0 %

This is a smooth, white, opaque glaze that doesn't move during firing. It may crawl if thick in corners or pinhole over rough-trimmed surfaces. Add ½–3 tsp. Epsom salts to 5 gallons of glaze to flocculate if needed (for less settling and better application). Colorants with flux are usually applied in a thin wash to the raw glaze surface. Fire with a small 03 cone in the sitter to give a large cone 04 tipped to about 2–3 o'clock in front of the peep hole.

NON-REFRACTORY COLORANTS

Colorant	1 part
Frit	1 part
Bentonite	1 part

Add: Blue-green: Copper
    Blue: Cobalt
    Brown to plum (with Ferro frit 3110): Manganese
    Brown: Iron

REFRACTORY COLORANTS

Colorant	1 part
Frit	3-4 parts
Bentonite	½–1 part

Add: Grass green: Chrome
    Rusty orange: Rutile
    Ivory: Titanium Dioxide

Most stains are refractory enough to require this ratio: 1 part colorant, 3–4 parts frit, ½–1 part bentonite:

Body stains, like Mason 6020 manganese-alumina pink and Mason 6485 titanium yellow are too refractory for use on top of majolica, even with flux added. Refractory colorants that are not adequately fluxed will result in matte surfaces that are bumpy and/or pig-skinned (crinkled). Testing is the only way to really know.

SOLUBLE COLORANTS

Blue: Cobalt Sulfate
Turquoise: Copper Sulfate
Plummy brown: Manganese Chloride
Green: Chrome Chloride

- All soluble colorants are toxic raw.
- Do not inhale or ingest.
- Absorption hazards: do not handle without gloves.
- Soluble colorants are dissolved, rather than suspended, in water, so they wick into the surface of the ware with the water, making a very uniform ground color with a soft edge.
- If you want white areas, or to retain clean edges, wax areas before applying soluble colorants.
- Over-wetting the glaze when applying solubles may move raw glaze and cause color to migrate through the pot wall and/or cause crawling.
- Too much water on the raw glaze may also cause crawling in the fired glaze.

COMMERCIAL COLORANTS

Some single-coat commercial underglazes work for decorating on top of a majolica base glaze, while others are too refractory. Testing is the only way to determine which ones work. Several companies now make very nice pre-mixed majolica decorating colors. These colors are generally a combination of stains, flux, and vehicles, and they brush well.

Tall Ewer: Grey with Fruit, 12¼ inches (31 cm) in height, terra cotta with majolica glazes, fired to cone 04.

Specialized Techniques
MAJOLICA WITH LUSTERS

by Liz Quackenbush

Four-lobed dish with gold, 14½ inches (37 cm) in length, red earthenware, maiolica glaze, luster. 6

I apply all of my glazes to bisque ware with a brush. They need to be painted on in very liquid strokes, never allowing the brush to dry out during application. To avoid thin spots, which can resemble spilled milk after the firing, the glaze must be applied in a number of coats that, together, are the even thickness of a dime or a little thicker. I test this thickness by pushing my fingernail through the glaze to the clay body. Another way to avoid the look of a thin glaze coat is to apply a coat of white slip to the leather-hard clay wherever you plan to glaze.

After the glaze is applied, let it dry on the pot and then gently rub the surface with your fingertip and, while wearing a dust mask, and working outside or in a ventilated spray booth, use compressed air to blow off the dust. Rubbing the glaze surface helps to break up any air bubbles and decreases the potential for pin-holing.

Once the glaze is applied and rubbed down, it is ready for you to paint on. I start by planning out my decoration in pencil—the pencil lines will

Cosmic Dinnerware, 12½ inches (32 cm) in length (dinner plate), 8½ inches (22 cm) in length (salad plate), red earthenware, maiolica glaze, lusters, glass enamels.

Specialized Techniques

Lunar plates, 7½ inches (19 cm) in diameter, red earthenware, maiolica glaze, luster.

burn out during the glaze firing. Once the design is laid out, I start to paint using coloring oxides and stains mixed with Gerstley borate.

After the glaze firing, I apply the lusters using a clean brush that's dedicated to luster use. The fumes given off by the luster are very dangerous so you should always wear rubber gloves and an appropriate vapor mask (or properly fitted respirator) and work in a well-ventilated area when using them. If the luster gets too thick to brush on smoothly, thin it with a drop of turpentine. To clean your brushes, use turpentine, followed by soap and water. Fire the luster decoration to cone 017 in a well-ventilated kiln.

Last, I add vivid color using fired on glass enamels made by Reusche (www.reuscheco.com). Most colors can be painted on in one layer, but some get muddy unless they are painted on in many thin layers with a firing in between each layer. This process can take time, but multiple firings can achieve vibrant colors. Slowly layering materials and imagery also allows the piece to evolve organically.

Plate with coins, 9 inches (23 cm) in diameter, red earthenware, maiolica glaze, glass enamels. 3 *Lunar* plates, 7½ inches (19 cm) in diameter, red earthenware, maiolica glaze, luster.

Glazing Techniques

MAIOLICA GLAZE
Cone 04

Ferro Frit 3110	9.6 %
Ferro Frit 3124	66.9
Ball Clay (OM4)	6.8
Silica	16.7
	100.0 %
Bentonite	4.8 %
Zircopax	9.6 %

This glaze needs to be mixed into a very thick solution. Add only enough water to make it the consistency of a melted milkshake. If too thin, it will sink to the bottom of the bucket and harden like a rock! The glaze should be fired to a hot cone 04. The glaze needs to be cooled slowly so I down fire from 1100°F to 400°F, decreasing no faster than 150°F per hour.

OVERGLAZE COLORS
Cone 04

I use cobalt carbonate for blue, copper carbonate for green, manganese dioxide for brown, and green chrome oxide for a forest green. These colors are mixed with water and painted on top of the white maiolica base glaze. Other colors can be achieved by using Mason or Degussa stains. They should be mixed with Gerstley borate in a ratio of 1 part stain to 3–4 parts Gerstley borate (by volume). If a color appears dry after firing, add more Gerstley borate to help melt the color.

GLASS ENAMELS
Cone 021

Reusche brand (www.reuscheco.com) glass enamels come in many colors. They are powders and need to be mixed with a medium before use. For the medium, I use a mixture of 1 part antifreeze with 3 parts water (by volume). I scoop a spoonful of the powdered enamel on to a pane of glass, add a small amount of medium, and mash it with a pallet knife until it forms an evenly thick paste. At this point, I put the medium away and only add water if needed. Even if it drys out, I only add water to moisten this mixture after the original paste is made. The enamels are painted on to the glaze-fired surface and fired to cone 021.

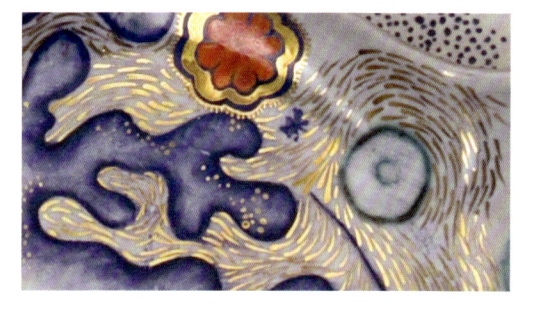

Chicken covered dish, 10 inches (25 cm) in length, earthenware, maiolica glaze, overglaze, luster.

Porcupine, 8 inches (20 cm) in length, red earthenware, maiolica glaze, luster, glass enamels.

Specialized Techniques
THE MAJOLICA OF POSEY BACOPOULOS

by Clay Cunningham

Posey Bacopoulos's majolica techniques begins with any leather-hard or bone dry pot made from earthenware clay (Posey uses Stan's Red from Highwater Clay). Before bisque firing, a thin layer of red terra sigillata is painted onto the foot of the pot, as well as any places that are to remain unglazed (figure 1). This creates a nice, rich shine to the exposed clay, and also helps to create a watertight surface on the pot. When the pot is bone dry fire it to cone 05½ on a slow cycle.

Glaze the bisqued pot with the PB Matte Majolica Glaze. Mix the glaze to a consistency slightly thicker than 'normal' glaze thickness. Smaller forms can be dipped using glazing tongs while for larger forms such as the one in this demonstration, the glaze needs to be poured and dipped. Pour the glaze into the pot's interior and dip it onto the exterior (figure 2). Take care to keep the glaze from overlapping too excessively. Heavily overlapped majolica glaze shows the discrepancies of thickness after firing and could crawl or pinhole if too thick.

With a sponge, wipe the foot of the pot thoroughly clean. If making a lidded vessel, remove the glaze on the rim of the pot and the underside of the lid with a sponge to avoid the lid sticking to the pot in the kiln (figure 3). After the glaze dries, smooth out any air bubbles, drips, or pinholes by gently rubbing the surface and dusting off the loosened material. Use a mask or respirator when rubbing or blowing the glaze dust.

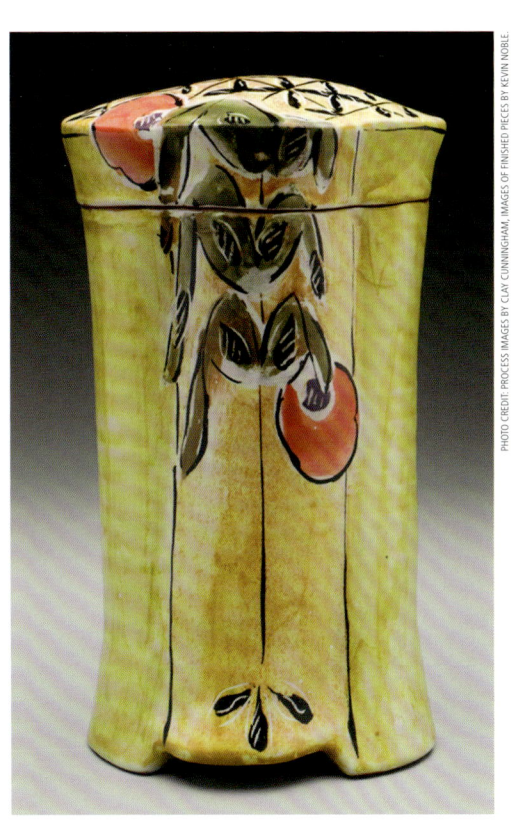

Tall oval box, 8 inches (20 cm) in height, earthenware, with majolica base glaze and overglaze stains.

Inglaze Decoration

Once the piece has 'cured' for a day, it is time to decorate! Begin by using a soft #2 pencil to lightly draw out the decoration (figure 4). Using the pencil first allows you to run through ideas before committing fully with the brush and stains. Decoration can be as minimal as a few dots of color or as elaborate as an overall pattern covering the piece. The choice is up to you. If you make a mistake, it can be gently 'erased' with a finger.

Unlike painting, where the background is usually painted on first, the majolica technique begins with painting the foreground using a stain paste

Glazing Techniques

1. Apply terra sigillata to the lid of the bone dry piece.
Process images by Clay Cunningham

2. Dip the exterior, and smooth out any overlaps with your finger.

3. Clean the lip, lid, and foot with a sponge.

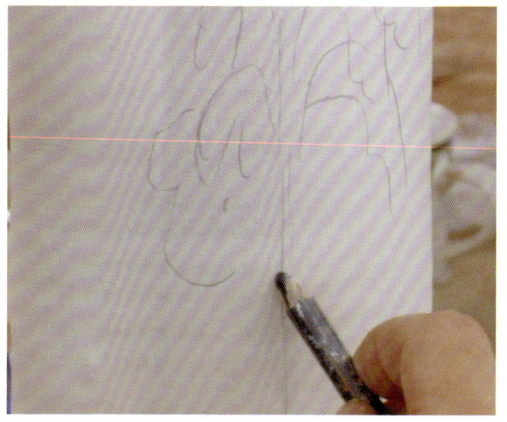

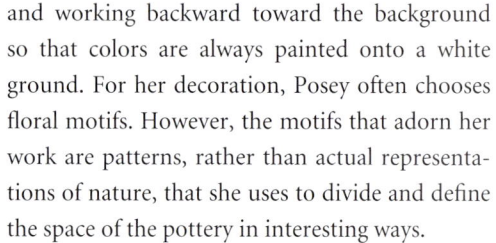

4. Draw on the design over the glaze with a pencil first.

and working backward toward the background so that colors are always painted onto a white ground. For her decoration, Posey often chooses floral motifs. However, the motifs that adorn her work are patterns, rather than actual representations of nature, that she uses to divide and define the space of the pottery in interesting ways.

Mix the stain paste to a thinned glaze consistency. If it's too watery, it may drip or run down the side of your pot. Too thick, and the brush will not glide easily across the raw glaze surface. Starting with the foreground, apply the stain pastes with a brush. Posey uses a Marx 5 Long Dagger brush which is perfect for long, flowing lines with varied thickness. To create an added layer of interest to your decoration, load your brush by first dipping it into one color and then dabbing a second color onto the tip. When the brush moves across the surface of the pot, the colors gracefully blend together. Loading the brush can add an element of depth and interest to your brushwork.

To boldly outline your shapes, apply a smooth coat of black stain or paste with a Marx Dagger 636 brush (figure 5). Deemed by Posey as the "Magic Brush," this brush is angled at the tip which allows for great line variance as you move it. With practice, beautiful flowing lines are possible. The black lining around the shapes helps to define it from the rest of the pot, as well as creating a dark color on which to carve back through. Known as sgraffito, the process of scratching through the black outline to the white glaze underneath is a great technique to help define a shape or to add a little extra decoration (figure 6). Though any semi-

Specialized Techniques

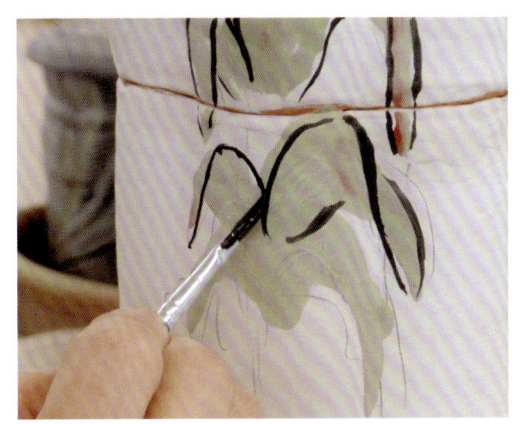

5. Outline the floral foreground with black stain.

6. Use a stylus for creating sgraffito decoration.

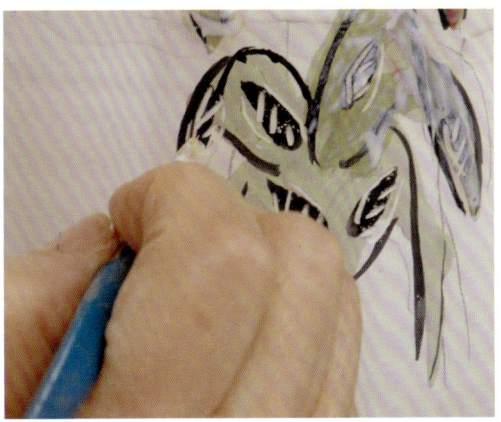

7. Coat the foreground with wax resist.

8. Designing a 'blossom' with a finger.

sharp object can be used for sgraffito, avoid using objects that are very sharp or thin, such as a needle tool, as they make lines that are too skinny and offer very little line variance. Posey recommends and uses a Kemper Wire Stylus WS.

After finishing all the foreground decoration, it's time to start working toward the background. Instead of painting the middle ground and background color around the shapes painted on the pot, which can hinder the fluidity and evenness of your background, Posey prefers to wax resist her foreground decoration. Apply a thin coat of wax resist directly over the decoration (figure 7). (Note: Even though the wax is dry, allow it to cure for twenty-four hours before touching it with your hands. If it is still damp, it may stick to your fingers and thus pull the stain decora-

tion off. However, the sponge is safe to use on the waxed areas.) Once dry, the middle ground and then the background color can be applied directly onto the entire pot and voila, the wax prevents the new stain from absorbing into the glazed pot. If the wax goes outside of the decoration's border, don't worry. A thin white line surrounding the decoration can add a loose, gestural quality to the piece.

Since the foremost decoration is already painted and now waxed, any new overglaze colors brushed over will appear to be directly behind the initial drawings, thus creating a middle ground. Posey uses her finger to dab additional color, for example, creating the center of a 'blossom' (figure 8). The blossoms are then elaborated upon with brushwork (figure 9). Once this decoration has

115

Glazing Techniques

9. Pull handle-like forms and attach the feet to the bottom of the main volume.

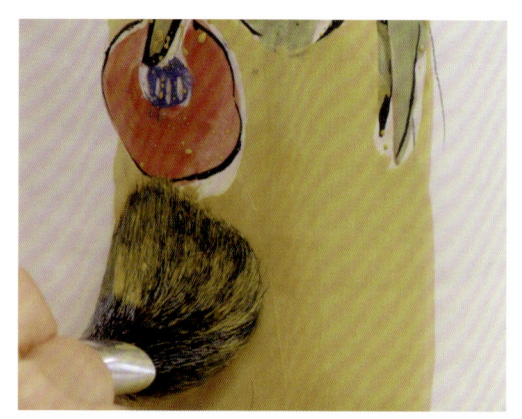

10. Dart, fold in, and join the top of the main volume. Cut a small circle in the top for stems to fit through.

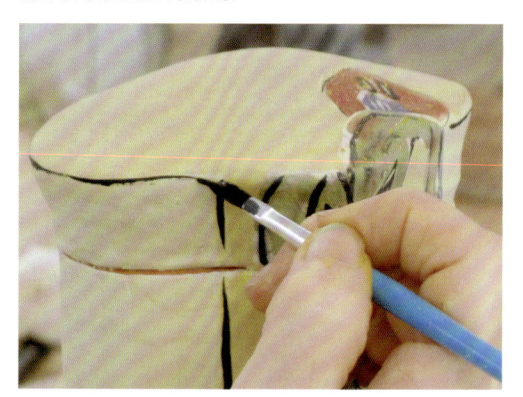

11. Form a thinner, taller cylinder for the top tier and cut darts to form the top.

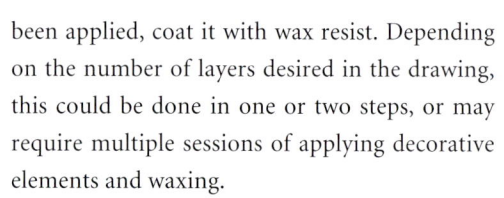

12. Cut a square from the top following the grid lines and clean and smooth the edges.

been applied, coat it with wax resist. Depending on the number of layers desired in the drawing, this could be done in one or two steps, or may require multiple sessions of applying decorative elements and waxing.

Once all individual objects of decoration are painted on and protected with wax resist, it's time to give the rest of the piece an overall hue. Though it can be left white, Posey prefers to liven up the surface with a uniting color. To apply the background color, Posey uses a Loew-Cornell 275 brush as it can hold a large amount of stain paste and creates a nice, wide swath of color (figure 10). Here she brushes vanadium stain paste onto the piece directly over her previous decoration. The entire surface can be colored or the decoration can be painted in any manner or pattern to design the background. To add variety to the surface, a small atomizer filled with rutile stain paste can be sprayed onto the surface (figure 11). This allows for a varied and mildly textured surface similar to pottery fired in atmospheric kilns. After applying the background, use a small damp sponge and carefully wipe over the waxed decoration to remove any beads of residual glaze.

Finishing and Firing

With the entire piece colored, any additional decoration can be added on top of the background color using the black stain or paste (figure 12). Here Posey paints on a grid design which adds additional patterning as well as helping to compose the space within the form of the pot. As before, sgraffito can be used to add variety to lines or for further decoration (figure 13). Don't forget

13. Add sgraffito work on the lid to match the jar.

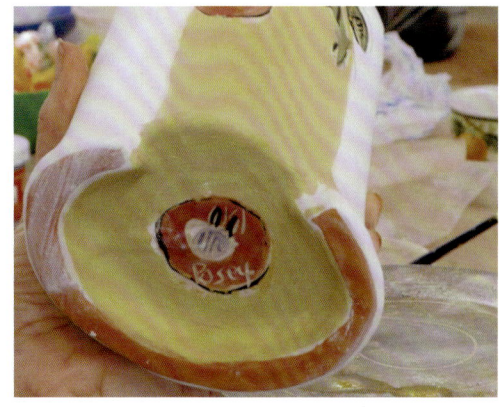

14. Drawings included on the bottom of the pot.

15. Add stain paste base to the colorant, 3½ parts paste to 1 part colorant by volume.

16. Mix the stain to the consistency of peanut butter.

the foot and the inside of the pot. Adding small, yet similar, decoration to the inside of your pottery helps relate all the parts of the work to one another, and gives the viewer an additional 'surprise' to find later (figure 14).

Load the glazed piece into the electric kiln and fire to cone 05. Fire the kiln slowly, particularly in the latter stage of the firing, for a total time of no less than twelve hours. This allows the glaze to even out and allows any additional gasses in the clay to burn off slowly, ensuring that your colors are even and free from pinholes. The good news is that majolica glazes are typically very stable, meaning they won't run. Not only does that mean that you won't have any glaze to grind off the bottom of your pot, your decoration won't run either.

Glaze Materials

Though most surface treatments can be adapted to work in more than one firing range, terra sigillata and majolica techniques are primarily intended only for low-fire. Using terra sigillata creates a satiny smooth and more water-tight surface for the majolica decorating technique.

Terra Sigillata

Terra sigillata is an ultra-refined slip that can be applied to bone dry (or bisque fired) clay. When brushed onto bone-dry wares, the extreme fineness of the platelets in the terra sig causes them to naturally lay flat on the surface, resulting in a smooth, satiny coating, even with just a very thin translucent layer. If the terra sig is polished when still slightly damp with a soft cloth, the pad of your finger, or a thin piece plastic, it will give a high gloss without heavy burnishing. Terra sig will not run or stick to other pieces in the kiln or to a kiln shelf. It works best at low temperatures including pit and barrel firing, but can be fired higher with adjustments to the mix.

Making Terra Sigillata

Terra sig can be made from any clay, though some have a smaller particle size and will have a greater yield. No matter what clay you use, in order for terra sig to settle properly, it must be deflocculated, which makes the particles repel one another and keeps the finest particles in suspension. To achieve the best results, use a combination of 1 part sodium silicate and 1 part soda ash, based on the dry weight of clay. Weigh out the deflocculant and dissolve thoroughly in hot water (already measured into a larger container). Slowly add the desired clay and blend thoroughly with a mixer or a large wire whisk. (Red or white earthenware can be used and colorants can be added to both after the middle layer is extracted). Allow the terra sig to sit undisturbed for several days or until three distinct layers become visible. Delicately remove the middle layer using a ball syringe or similar device, being careful not to overly disturb the mixture as a whole. This middle layer is the terra sig. Put it in a separate container for use. The top layer will be mostly water and the bottom layer will essentially be sludge, both can be discarded. The sig layer is now ready for use or can be colored if desired, generally 1 cup of sig to 1 tbsp. of stain.

Majolica Stain Pastes

Majolica stains are made with frits and/or Gerstley borate, which are fluxes and glass formers. They allow the stain pastes to melt into the white base majolica glaze they are layered on top of and add to an overall and consistent glossy finish. Majolica is a low-fire technique, you can use any commercial stain or coloring oxide to achieve the color you want. Test recipes before using them on finished work, and always wear a respirator.

TOASTY RED BROWN TERRA SIGILLATA
Cone 05

Water	14 cups
Red Art Clay	1,500 g
Sodium Silicate	1 tsp

Mix thoroughly and allow to settle into three distinct parts. Pour off the top, thinnest layer. Pour the remaining liquid (middle layer) into a lidded container to use as your terra sigillata. Discard the bottom sludge. Use on leather-hard or bone dry ware.

PB MATTE MAJOLICA
Cone 05

Ferro Frit 3124	65 %
EPK Kaolin	20
Dolomite	10
Silica	5
Total	100 %
Add: Zircopax	10%

Epsom salts solution: Put water into a mixing container and add dry ingredients. Once settled, stir vigorously while adding a saturated Epsom salt solution (approximately 1 tsp. per 1000 gram batch). Add water to achieve a thick, creamy consistency slightly thicker than a typical glaze. To make a saturated Epsom salt solution, mix Epsom salts into a cup of water until no more will dissolve.

STAIN PASTE BASE
Cone 05

Ferro Frit 3124	50 %
Gerstley Borate	50
Total	100 %

Mix by volume. This is the base recipe for making colors to paint on over the base glaze. For commercial stains, the ratio should be 3½ parts Stain Paste Base to 1 part colorant by volume (figure 15). Most commercial stains will work, but test first.

Green:	Mason Florentine Green 6202
	Mason Bermuda Green 6242
Blue:	Mason Navy Blue 6386
Yellow:	Mason Vanadium Yellow 6404
Purple:	Mason Pansy Purple 6385
Chartreuse:	Mason Chartreuse 6236
Brown:	Mason Chocolate Brown 6124
Gray:	Mason Charcoal Grey 6528
Black:	Duncan EZ Stroke Black EZ012

For oxides, mix 1 part Stain Paste Base to 1 part oxide by volume.

Brown:	Red Iron Oxide
Turquoise:	Copper Carbonate

For Stain Pastes, mix to the consistency of creamy peanut butter (figure 16) and thin as needed for brushing.

Specialized Techniques
CHINA PAINTING BASICS

by Paul Lewing

There are four temperature ranges clay artists typically fire to: high-fire (cone 8-12), mid-range (cone 4-6), low-fire (cone 06-04), and china paint (cone 018-015). Materials designed for the lowest firing range—china paints, overglaze enamels and lusters—behave more like paint than any other ceramic medium. For clay artists like me, who came to clay from painting, however, using china paint specifically is a real treat.

A Few Facts

You can think of china paint as essentially a very thin, very low-temperature glaze that's almost always applied over a fired glazed surface. In fact, it's so thin that it takes on the surface characteristics of the glaze it's put over; for example, applied on a glossy glaze, it will be shinier than over a matte glaze.

Some people make a distinction between china paint and overglaze enamel, stating that china paints are transparent while overglaze enamels are opaque. But they're basically the same things and are both fired at the same temperatures.

One of the advantages of china paint is that the colors are the same before firing as after, unlike many glazes. The biggest difference is that there are three groups of china paint colors, and they're not intermixable. One group includes the cadmium reds, oranges, and some of the yellows; the second includes the gold, purples, pinks and lavenders; and the last includes all the other colors.

Glazing Techniques

Here is the first coat on a tile mural project. Care has been taken to keep colors from overlapping since most china paints are not intermixable.

One of the advantages of china paints is that the colors are the same before firing as after.

Colors are often applied in layers. Here the mural has had more china paints applied to add intensity and shading then fired a second time.

Mural detail.

If you try to mix, for instance, a cadmium red with a non-cadmium yellow, you won't get orange. You get a bubbly ugly brown.

Traditionally, these color groups are fired to different temperatures. The gold group is usually fired first, to cone 015, then the everything-else group to cone 017 or 016, and the cadmium group last, to cone 018. Colors are often applied in layers, in multiple firings at each temperature, to build up intensity. Sometimes you can fire a color from one group then add a color from another group in a subsequent firing, but it depends on which color is first.

China paints are traditionally applied using a mineral oil medium. They can be bought already mixed with oil, or as a dry powder. Amaco also makes an overglaze enamel called Versacolor, which is available as either oil- or water-based.

Using China Paints

I never had any lessons in china painting or read any books on it, so I just made up my own technology, and I do a number of things that would horrify a traditional china painter who follows the guidelines. For one thing, I use water as a medium. This would be a problem if I worked on vertical surfaces, but since I only paint tile, I can pile on a much thicker coat without it running.

Second, I fire all the colors to cone 016. This seems to work fine, and I just can't think about firing all the purples in a mural in one firing and the reds in another.

Dinner, 22 inches high by 58 inches long.

Hopi pattern, 6-inch-square tiles, silk screen printed china painted for tub surround.

Lastly, I don't have time to do the dozens of firings on each piece that a traditionalist would do. On a typical tile mural, I do three firings. The first establishes the background colors, the second adds intensity and shading, and the third adds black outlines. Some people do the outlines first, but I think it makes crisper outlines to do them last.

I use all the brushes and techniques I learned for watercolor to apply china paint. I start by dumping some dry powder onto a palette and mixing in water a drop at a time with a rubber bulb. I can make thin washes or a thick paste. If I decide I don't want the brush marks, I blot with a stencil brush or a small piece of foam rubber. Traditional china painters use a wad of cotton in a piece of silk. Another technique, called pouncing (used to get intense, even color), is done by coating the area to be painted with a sticky oil, and dumping dry powder on with a shaker or mop brush. The excess is then knocked or blown off.

Painting on a slick surface is quite different from painting on absorbent bisque or raw glaze, but one big advantage is that you can wipe it off and start over. Tools made of foam, rubber or wood work well to remove color in selected areas.

Some Advanced Techniques

When I need to spray china paint for a large, even color area, the water-based medium on a slick surface is a problem. So I first spray the area with a fairly thick solution of cornstarch and water, then dry it with a hair dryer. When a solution of color and water is sprayed over this, it stays without beading up.

I also silk-screen china paint. You can silk-screen any substance that will go through your screen as long as it will not dry quickly and if you can mix it to a consistency similar to mayonnaise. You can't print one color over another without firing in between, but you can print colors next to each other. To do this, you will need a medium that will dry fairly hard in a reasonable time, but will still wash out of your screen when it's dry. Potterycraft used to make a product in a tube that was perfect for this, and I've tried many other substances as a substitute. For single colors, ethylene glycol works well, but it never dries, so you can't put a screen down on it for a second color. I'm now using a mixture of water and gum arabic, about half-and-half, and then I mix in dry powder to get the right consistency.

Silk-screening must be done on a flat surface, but printing on tile is just like printing on paper, except for the substance you put through the screen. Take a class or buy a kit to learn how. For printing on non-flat surfaces, you need to make decals. Commercial ceramic decals are made using china paints.

I use a process for making screens that's manufactured by Hun-Speedball, and available in art supply stores. It's a light-based system, but doesn't require a darkroom or careful control of water temperatures. Instructions come with the chemicals, and it makes screens that are usable with either water or oil. I use 12XX mesh screen, which is a medium mesh size.

WARNING: Since china paints melt at such a low temperature, there is much less silica and alumina in them than in low-fire glazes. This means that harmful things like cadmium and lead are less bound up in the glaze, so china paints are definitely not for food-contact surfaces. All the precautions for ventilation and dust are doubly important, and they are not for children. There are lead-free china paints available, but most do contain lead. Some even contain arsenic.

Under heavy daily use, china paints will wear off, as they have on your grandmother's everyday china, but for decorative objects and tile, even in showers, the durability is fine. If you want faster, cheaper firings, brighter colors, and more painterly effects than even low-fire glazes or underglazes produce, go as low as you can go—try china paints.

Reef, 6½ feet in height by 14 feet in length. China-painted tile.

Specialized Techniques
USING LUSTERS

by Jonathan Kaplan

Ceramic artist Barbara Davis Schwartz is an expert in using ceramic lusters over glazed surfaces. Lusters for ceramics have been associated with one of the final finishing steps that you would see with commercial dinnerware, often as bands of gold, silver or platinum applied on the rims of plates.

Barbara uses combinations of luster preparations. Over many years of testing and researching, she has developed a multi-layering and multi-firing approach.

A Luster Primer

What are lusters? You've probably seen small bottles of lusters at your ceramic supplier, usually stored behind the counter. Lusters come in small glass bottles ranging from 5–100 grams. They have names such as "Liquid Bright Gold," "Mother of Pearl," "Opal Luster," or "Carmine Luster," just to mention a few. These materials are combinations of metals, some of them precious, suspended in resins and binders that are applied over a glazed surface. They're fired at a very low temperature, usually in the range of cone 022–017, and result in a thin film of metal that reflects and refracts light waves differently.

The color of the glaze and the type glaze surface they rest on top of also affect how the luster appears. For instance, an application of Mother of Pearl luster leaves a very thin coating of metal, usually tin, that resembles an oil slick—a colorful rainbow of color. If used over a clear glaze on a porcelain clay body, that clear glaze then resembles a multi-hued spectrum of colors. On a matte glaze, the luster surface will be dull. These colors will be different from each viewing angle and change depending on the type of light in the room. If a layer of Liquid Bright Gold or Platinum is used, there will be a thin layer of that precious metal fused or bonded onto the glazed surface beneath it.

Altered Vessel #24, 10½ inches (27 cm) in height, porcelain fired to cone 6 in oxidation, handpainted, multi-layered and multi-fired lusters.

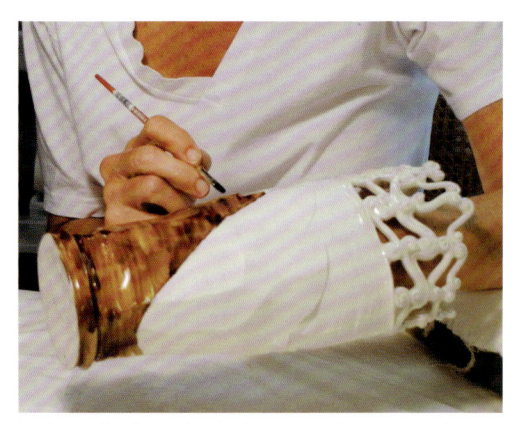

1. Apply the luster in single non-overlapping strokes.

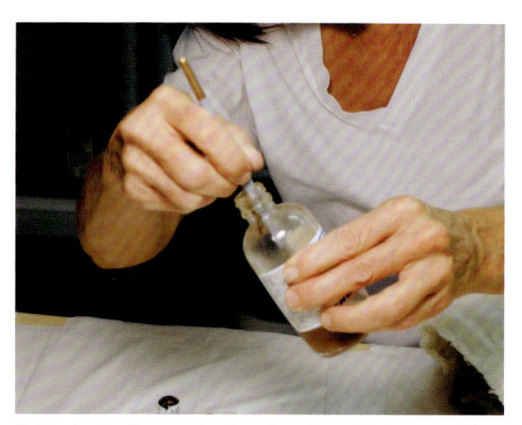

2. Use Luster Essence to clean brushes with luster residue.

Safety Issues
- Lusters are not glazes and are therefore not durable. They should never be used on the interior of any vessel intended for food or beverage.
- Lusters and solvents are very flammable. Never use any of these materials close to sparks or open flames.
- Dispose of any solvent rags in specially designed flameproof containers. These can be purchased from any industrial supplier.
- Always wear a respirator when the luster bottles are open, when using lusters, when firing lusters, and when cleaning brushes.
- Wear rubber gloves when working with lusters.

A Clean Studio
After creating and glaze firing her porcelain pieces, Barbara prepares her studio to use luster. She begins by making sure that her studio is spotlessly clean. Any dust that falls onto a freshly lustered piece can cause a defect in the fired surface. She cleans and re-covers her worktable, mops the floor, and clears the clutter from the table. Her brushes are stored vertically in jars with their handles pointing down, separated by type. Her small bottles of lusters are also well organized.

Barbara follows several important rules when working with lusters in her studio to protect herself and her work: adequate ventilation, cleanliness, no food, no hand lotion, and no putting the brush in her mouth.

Preparing the Work
Barbara cleans her pieces with denatured alcohol and a clean cotton cloth. Denatured alcohol leaves no residue on the piece and removes any trace of oils from your skin. After cleaning the surface, used cloths are discarded into a flameproof container designed for flammable material disposal.

She then uses a felt marker to delineate the sections of the piece where the gold luster will be applied. It's possible to use an airbrush to apply ceramic luster but she prefers to brush the surface in order to control the quantity of luster used. Spraying consumes more material and the precious metals are too expensive to waste if oversprayed.

Applying Lusters
Barbara pours out a small quantity of gold luster into a reusable porcelain palette or tray. Dipping her brush into the luster, she begins to apply it onto the glaze-fired piece with even brush strokes. She works methodically, moving the brush in only one direction and doesn't go over any previous brush strokes in an attempt to even out the layer of luster—it does so on its own as it dries (figure 1). Using the same brush, she then returns the unused luster from the palette back into the bottle. With the first step completed, she waits about an hour before the applying the marbleizing liquid.

Brush Cleaning and Maintenance
Luster essence is used to clean and condition the

Specialized Techniques

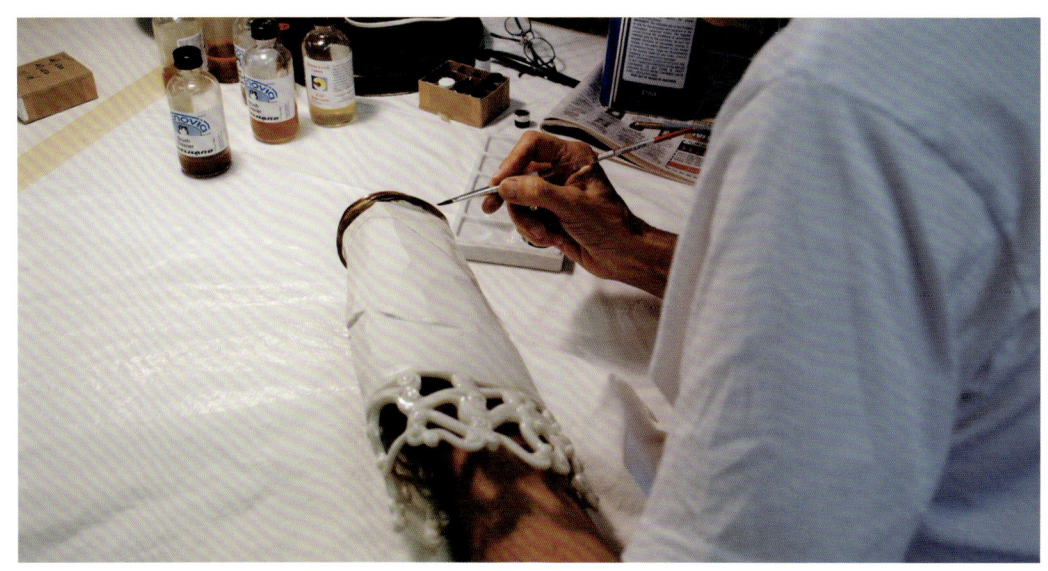

3. Detail of the three bottles of Essence used for cleaning.

4. Test tiles of luster layering and marbleizing.

5. Apply the Marbleizing Liquid in broad strokes with a flat brush in a single layer.

brushes (figure 2). Barbara has three bottles of Luster Essence she uses to remove the material from the brushes. The majority of the luster is removed in the first bottle. After drying the brush with a cotton cloth, she then cleans the brush again in the second bottle, repeating the drying and final cleaning in the last bottle. The liquid in the last bottle shows no sign of any metallic pigment residue (figure 3).

Marbleizing Application

Marbleizing Liquid is a low-strength solvent that's used to break up the surface tension of unfired gold luster into a network of fine multi-colored webbing. The degree of webbing and color depends on when it is applied over the first layer of Liquid Bright Gold. As you can see from her many test tiles (figure 4), there are many different resulting surfaces that can be achieved with the Marbleizing Liquid. Light is reflected differently over a marbleized surface and there is no set result. Everything about the final surface depends on the glaze and the glaze color. Generally, a dull or matte glaze will produce a dull luster surface. Conversely, a gloss glaze will yield a shiny luster. If the luster is applied over a black glaze, the light will reflect differently than it would if the luster was applied over a light colored or white surface. Lustering is

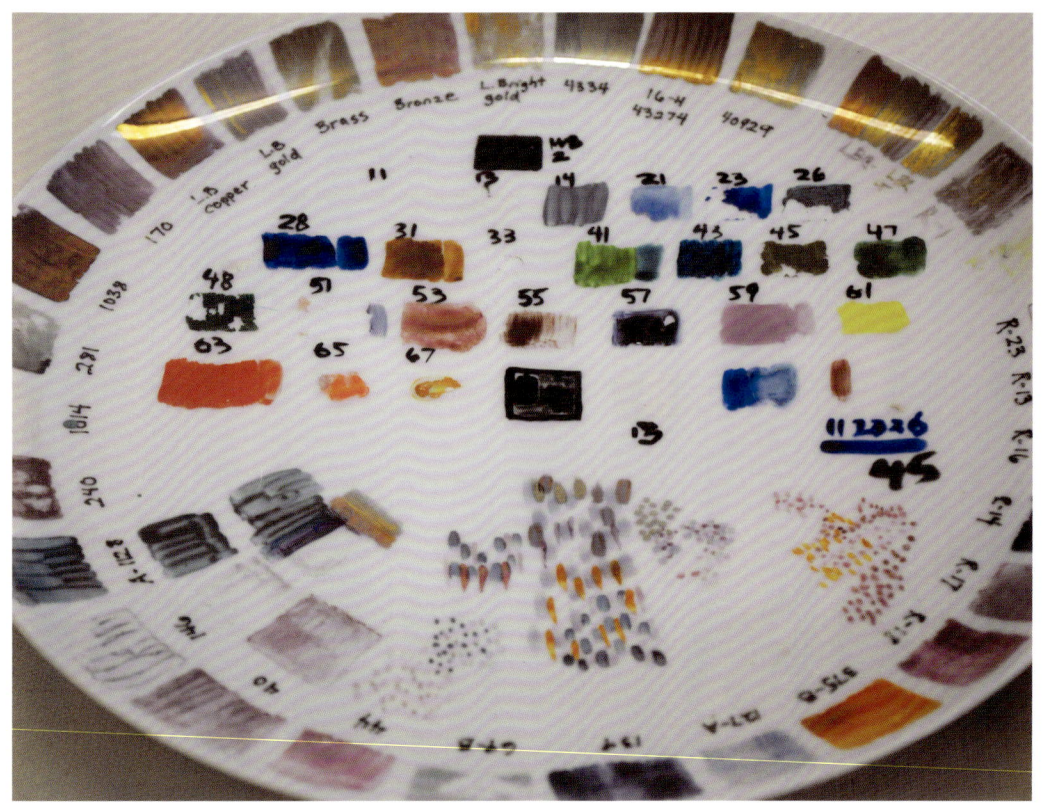

6. Individual luster tests on a commercial plate.

all about reflection and refraction, and using Marbleizing Liquid adds yet another dimension to this play of light.

Barbara applies the Marbleizing Liquid with a flat brush and a very light touch so that the liquid does not drag the earlier applied gold luster (figure 5). After applying an even coat, she lets the piece dry. Drying time can also affect the degree of webbing and patterning that the final firing will produce.

Firing

Fire the pieces in a well-ventilated kiln between cone 022–cone 018. When firing lusters, open the kiln door or prop the lid slightly as air is necessary to complete the burning out of organic matter at approximately 800°F. Temperature has a profound effect on the finished surface and Barbara has seen many different results so experiment to see which temperature works best for you.

Test Results

- Much like testing glazes to understand their application, properties and fired results, it's also necessary to test lusters. Barbara has tested hundreds of combinations of metallic pigments (figure 6) and has some suggestions that might be useful:
- Liquid Bright Gold, Platinum, and Palladium lusters are generally solid colors and work best as a first coat.
- Wait until the initial coat of these metals dries before applying a second coat of transparent or translucent lusters such as Mother of Pearl or any of the colored lusters.
- When using Marbleizing Liquid, experiment with timing the application of this material over the base layer.
- Apply lusters over any glazed surface. Transparent or translucent lusters will have a different appearance whether over matte or glossy glazes.

Specialized Techniques
COMBINING FIRED AND POST-FIRED SURFACES

by Magda Gluszek

Using paste and resin epoxies, oil paint, acrylic paint, chalk pastels, microfilament, candy sprinkles, paste wax, and other materials allows you to go beyond the fired surface to create unique surfaces.

My work takes advantage of both ceramic materials and mixed media when creating the confection-referencing surfaces. Along with traditional surface treatments like terra sigillata, glaze, and colored stains, I use paste and resin epoxies, oil paint, acrylic paint, chalk pastels, microfilament, candy sprinkles, paste wax, and other materials as they relate to my concepts.

Fired Finishes

When a figure I've created is nearly bone dry, I apply a coating of white terra sigillata to the legs and terra sigillata colored with pink Mason stain to the upper body (figure 1). The sculpture is bisque fired to cone 06.

After the bisque firing, I prepare several commercial stains with Gerstley borate and paint them in concentrated areas to accentuate the sprigging and stamps (figure 2). Excess stain is removed with a damp sponge. Three brush coats of red glaze are applied to the hair and the piece is fired to cone 03.

For the final firing, a satin matte glaze is mixed with several color variations and sieved through a 100 mesh screen. A few drops of sodium silicate deflocculate it and lessen the amount of water necessary to make it flow. This causes the glaze

Glazing Techniques

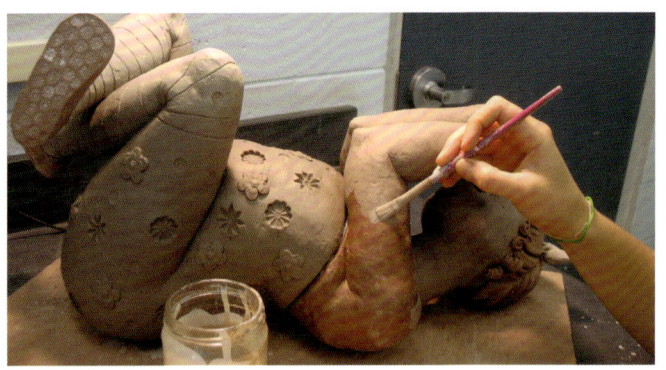

1. Apply white terra sigillata to the legs and pink terra sigillata to the upper body.

2. Brush the figure with a mixture of Gerstley borate and commercial stains.

to retain a raised quality when trailed over the form using an ear syringe fitted with an inflating needle (figure 3). Under-firing the glaze to cone 08 allows it to retain a raised, semi-matte quality, similar to icing.

Post-firing Finishes

When the glaze firing is done, I fit the figure with eyeballs. I prefabricate several porcelain eye shapes using Helios Porcelain from Highwater Clays, Inc., fire them separately to cone 7, and attach them postfiring. The contrasting clay bodies and separation of the eyes from the form creates a dramatic and realistic expression. I paint the eyes with oil paints, thinned with linseed oil. The iris color is chosen to match the figure's red hair, then other highlight colors are added. A needle tool is used to detail the iris by dragging through lighter values of paint and creating highlights.

While the paint is drying, I add resin to selected parts of the figure, coloring it to resemble sugary syrup. Wearing gloves and a respirator that protects against volatile organic fumes, I mix equal parts of resin and hardener, and stir vigorously. A coating is painted over the eyes to protect the oil paint and add luminosity. Fine shavings of chalk pastels can be added to tint the resin a variety of colors. I pour it into the figure's mouth as well as various indentations formed by the stamps (figure 4). Confectionery sprinkles are embedded into the resin for further decoration (figure 5). Small pieces of microfilament are placed between the figure's fingertips and mouth and coated with resin to give the illusion of dripping.

After the resin cures overnight, I mix a small amount of two-part East Valley Epoxy putty which

Specialized Techniques

3. Trail a satin-matte glaze that's mixed with a deflocculant to create raised, icing-like line patterns.

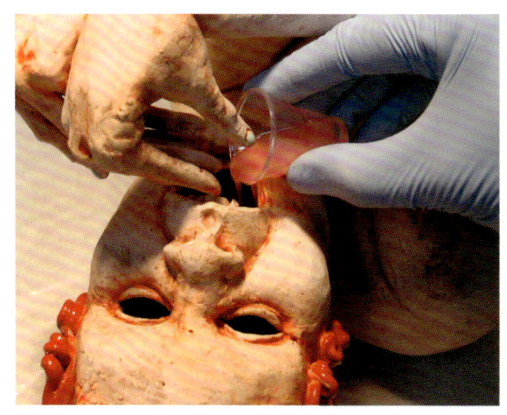

4. Mix epoxy resin with crushed chalk pastels to create the illusion of a sugary syrup.

5. Add confectionery sprinkles to the resin in the indented stamped area.

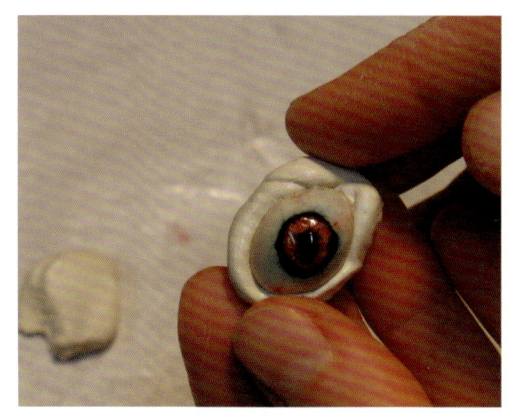

6. Apply epoxy putty around the eyeballs. This will secure them to the eye sockets.

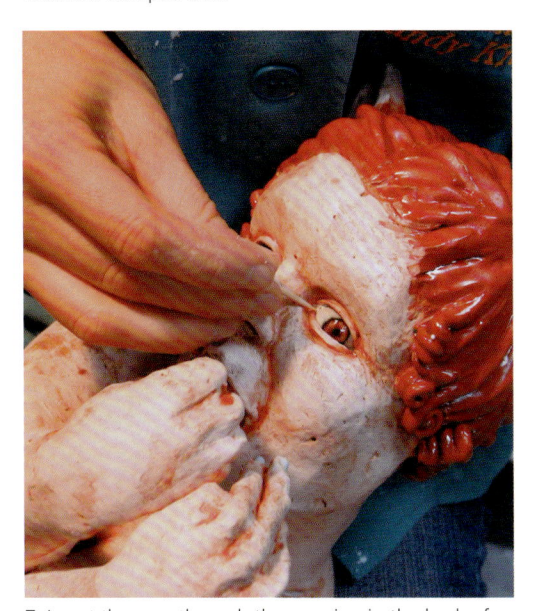

7. Insert the eyes through the opening in the back of the head and position them appropriately.

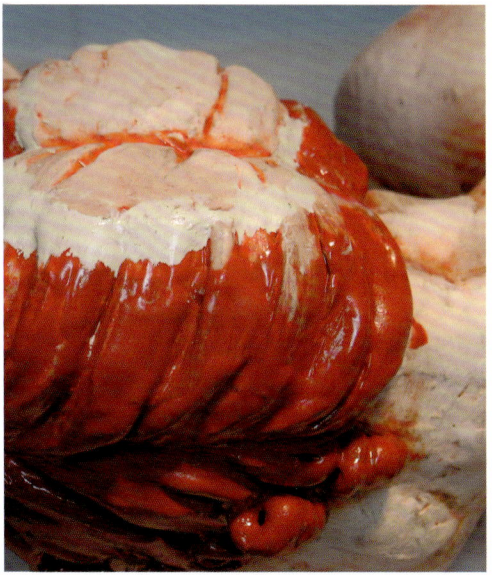

8. Epoxy the access point at the back of the head using epoxy putty.

129

Glazing Techniques

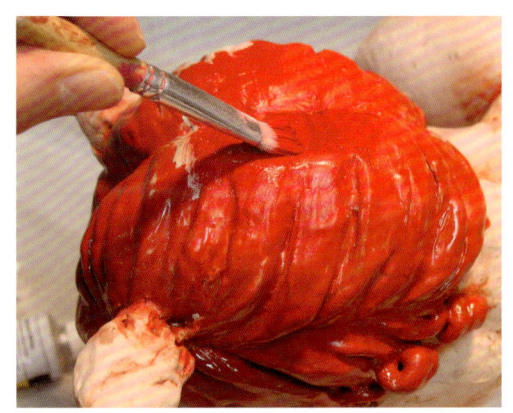

9. Disguise the repair using acrylic paint that's mixed to match the red glaze.

Magda's surface detail shows her seamless integration of traditional and multimedia decoration techniques.

can easily be modeled to mimic clay and apply it to the eyes (figure 6). They are carefully inserted into the sockets and positioned appropriately (figure 7). The figure is turned face-down while the epoxy cures, preventing the eyeballs from shifting. This allows me to attach the fired clay cover over the access point at the back of the head with more East Valley Epoxy putty and disguise the repair with acrylic paint (figures 8 and 9).

To complete the sculpture, a coating of paste wax is brushed on to the figure's flesh. When dry, it can be lightly buffed with a cloth to give the skin a soft sheen.

PETE PINNELL TERRA SIGILLATA

Water	3 cups
Dry Ball Clay (OM4)	400 g

Mix ingredients in a blender. Add sodium silicate drop by drop until the mix thins. Let sit for 48 hours. Keep the top 1/3 and discard remaining material.

PINK SIGILLATA

Terra Sigillata	1 cup
Mason Stain 6020 Pink	3 tsp

RED ICING GLAZE
Cone 03

Whiting	10 %
Ferro Frit 3124	50
Kona F-4 Feldspar	40
	100 %
Add: Mason Stain 6026 Lobster	25 %

COLORED STAIN

Mason Stain	1 part
Gerstley Borate	3 parts

Add: Green: MS 6242 Bermuda
      Blue: MS 6364 Turquoise Blue
      Red: MS 6026 Lobster
      Pink: MS 6020 Pink

VAL CUSHING TRANSPARENT SATIN GLAZE
Cone 03 (fired to Cone 06)

Gerstley Borate	17 %
Whiting	3
Ferro Frit 3124	52
Kona F-4 Feldspar	15
EPK Kaolin	2
Silica	11
	100 %
Add: Green: MS 6242 Bermuda	5 %
Blue: MS 6364 Turquoise Blue	5 %
Yellow: MS 6404 Vanadium	15 %

Specialized Techniques
AGED PATINA

by Philippe Faraut

On unglazed works, a wax finish is the best way to preserve the integrity of details, and provide some degree of protection against dust and stains.

Time has produced the rich, warm patina observed on ancient clay sculptures displayed in museums. The combination of years of dust, cleaning and handling has created surfaces that can look like leather, wood or stone depending on the original color of the earthenware. The clay busts produced centuries ago were sometimes glazed, but most were simply waxed. It was, and remains, the best way to preserve the integrity of details, and provide some degree of protection against dust and stains on unglazed ware. Through application of clay dust and wax, this technique creates the subtle look of ancient patinas without the wait.

Using different colors of clay dust on different clay bodies provides for a wide variety of tones. For example, a red clay sculpture with a light brown dusting of clay looks a little bit like wood, while a brown sculpture with a light white clay dust looks like leather. For a sculpture that would look like limestone (as shown here), I used white, low-fire earthenware clay for both the bust and the patina. The bust was fired to maturation (Cone 05). As a word of caution, you should always experiment on fired samples before attempting this type of patina on a valued piece, as it takes a little practice to achieve good results. Since this type of patina is somewhat translucent, your sculpture must be built carefully to prevent cracks during drying and firing. Any repairs done after firing might be visible through the wax.

Glazing Techniques

1. Rub damp rags against a block of clay until saturated. Hang in a warm place until bone dry.

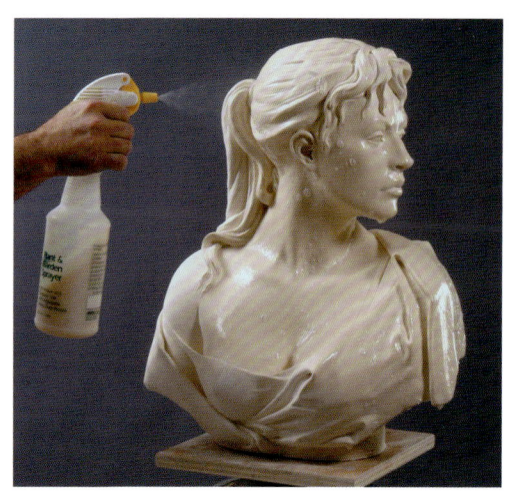

2. Spray floor wax over the entire piece

3. Immediately after spraying, slap one of the clay-loaded rags against the piece repeatedly.

4. When the desired look has been achieved, you need to spray a final layer of wax to obtain a satin finish.

Process

Rub four or five damp rags (white cotton T-shirts work best) against a block of wet clay until saturated. Hang in a warm place until rags and clay are bone dry (figure 1).

Spray Lundmark All-Wax Floor Wax over the entire piece (figure 2). Caution: Work outdoors or in a spray booth.

Immediately after spraying, slap one of the clay-loaded rags against the piece repeatedly until the right amount of dust sticks to the wax (figure 3).

A dust mask is required for this step. At first, this step can be unnerving because it sometimes looks blotchy. Add more wax until you are satisfied with the results. When the desired look has been achieved, you need to spray a final layer of wax to obtain a satin finish (figure 4).

Note: Lundmark All-Wax Floor Wax for asphalt tile, vinyl, linoleum, etc., is available from your local hardware store or it can be ordered online at www.doitbest.com.

Specialized Techniques
WORKING WITH SOLUBLE SALTS

by Diane Chin Lui

Beautiful, soft, muted-color brush strokes and washes of water-soluble metal salts decorate Gary Holt's translucent porcelain bowls and plates. The simplicity and quiet presence of his works belie the years that Holt spent experimenting and perfecting his technique. Using water-soluble metals salts (WSMS) demands excellent technical skills and careful attention to details.

Water-soluble metal salts are often compared to watercolors in application and decoration. They produce a variety of interesting effects on ceramic works, such as halos of color, fumed or smoky halos, solid shapes with soft, diffused edges or solid shapes with crisp sharp edges. They can be used to color terra sigillata and will not dull or matt the surface as oxides will.

Holt has been testing and experimenting with metal salts for more than twenty years, while running a successful pottery studio in Berkeley, California. With little research literature available on WSMS, he has had to develop his own techniques through trial and error.

Chemistry
Water-soluble metal salts are simple solutions that are composed of nitrate, chloride and sulfate forms of metals, which dissolve in water. They are simpler solutions in comparison to glazes, which are usually composed of fluxes, alumina and silica,

Latex resist was painted on the lip and underside of this porcelain vessel and 10% potassium dichromate was painted on the entire bowl. The latex was then removed and the following WSMS solutions were dotted and brushed on: 15% cobalt chloride, 50% cobalt chloride, 25% iron chloride, 50% nickel chloride and an "all gray" solution (10 grams each of potassium permanganate, cobalt chloride, molybdic acid and iron chloride in 100cc water).

as well as oxides, carbonates or stains, and which may contain metal elements. Metal carbonates and oxides are the most commonly used form of metals in glaze, but more than twenty water-soluble metal salts may also be used (see chart).

Application
Holt prefers to use Southern Ice porcelain, formulated by Australian ceramist Les Blakebrough. The plasticity of the clay compares to Limoges porcelain clay. It does not have bone ash as part of its body. Holt likes Southern Ice for its translucency and whiteness, and he has noted that the color of the clay affects the brightness or clarity of the met-

al salts. The darker the color of the clay body, the more muted the colors will be. As an alternative to porcelain, Holt suggests a white clay body, stoneware covered with white slip or plain stoneware.

Often the color may "sink" into the clay body, which may or may not be desirable. Holt applies an opaque glaze to the inside of a pot if he does not want the color to migrate to the other side of the wall. Also, to keep his metal salts on the surface of the wall longer, he uses a nonreactive thickener. The thickener has the added effect of intensifying the colors.

Firing

Holt states that the clay vessel or form must be bisque fired between applications of metal salts. This technique is called "setting" the color. All water-soluble metal salt colors are temperature sensitive. The colors will change depending on the firing temperature.

Practical and Safety Concerns

It is absolutely essential to observe safety and health precautions when using these materials. Holt refers to the Merck Index whenever he uses an unfamiliar material. As always, the potential hazards depend on the concentration of the chemicals used and the safety practices of the ceramist. Holt believes everyone can use WSMS with the required attention and care. A Materials Safety Data Sheet (MSDS) should accompany each product when purchased. If the supplier does not provide an MSDS, buyers should ask for one. These information sheets will provide the precautions for storing, using and disposing of the products.

Water-soluble metal salts should be stored in containers separate from regular glaze mixtures. The containers should be well labeled to avoid any accidental mixing of the chemicals. In addition, acids and bases should be kept in separate containers.

A NIOSH-approved respirator should be worn when measuring and working with water-soluble metal salts so the chemicals are not inhaled or ingested. Eye goggles should also be worn, es-

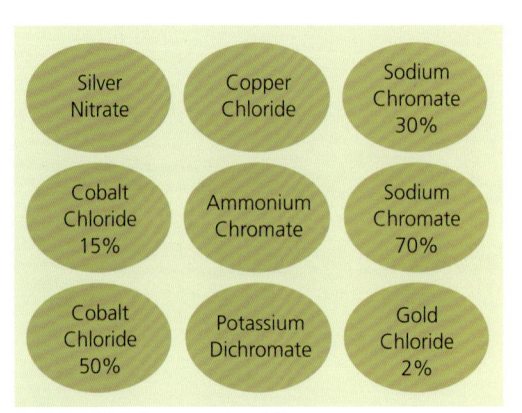

Silver Nitrate	Copper Chloride	Sodium Chromate 30%
Cobalt Chloride 15%	Ammonium Chromate	Sodium Chromate 70%
Cobalt Chloride 50%	Potassium Dichromate	Gold Chloride 2%

Key to WSMS Drops on Test Tiles

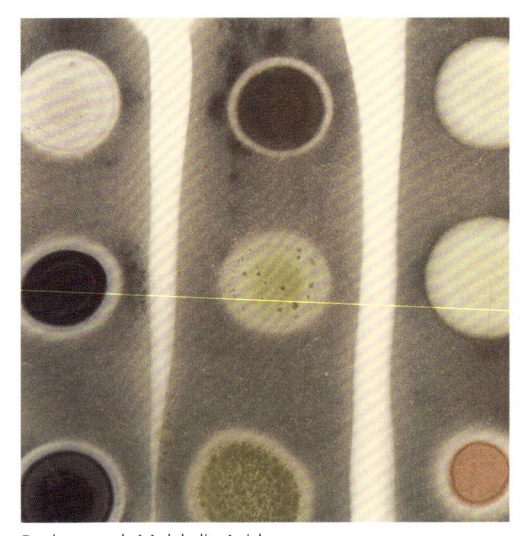

Background: Molybdic Acid

Background: Ammonium Chromate

Specialized Techniques

pecially when using acids. For hand protection, Holt wears two sets of gloves—a latex glove over a nitrile glove—because skin can easily absorb these chemicals.

Besides the health and safety concerns, local laws and regulations regarding the proper and safe disposal of the chemicals should be checked. When mixing the chemicals, Holt mixes only small amounts so that the disposal of the remaining solution is kept at a minimum.

Though the health and safety concerns are numerous and may appear overwhelming, they are necessary precautions to a rewarding and exciting facet of ceramics decoration that has been explored by few ceramists. Holt continues to experiment and add to his extensive body of knowledge on the subject and generously shares this knowledge through seminars and workshops. As evidenced by the fruits of Holt's experimentation, water-soluble metal salts present many possibilities for new forms of expression in ceramics.

WATER-SOLUBLE METAL SALT SOLUTIONS

For 5% solution
- Water-soluble metal salt . . . . 5 g
- Water 100ml

For 10% solution
- Water-soluble metal salt 10g
- Water 100ml

For 15% solution*
- Water-soluble metal salt 15g
- Water 100ml

As a rule of thumb
- 5% solution = light color
- 10%–15% solution = medium color
- 15% and above = intense color

Intensity of the color may be deepened by layering the color. However, most colors will not become darker once the surface is saturated with a 5% solution of the water-soluble metal salts.

*Potassium dichromate has a 12% maximum solution. More KCr^2 will not dissolve.

Water soluble metal salts are extremely toxic in the raw stage and should always be used following the utmost safety precautions. Carefully read and adhere to the guidelines on the following pages whenever using these salts.

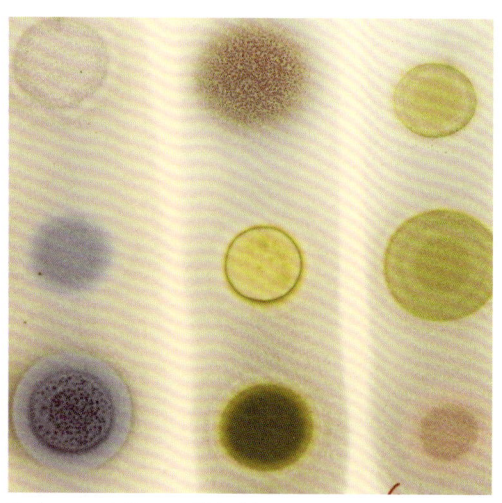

Background: Copper Chloride

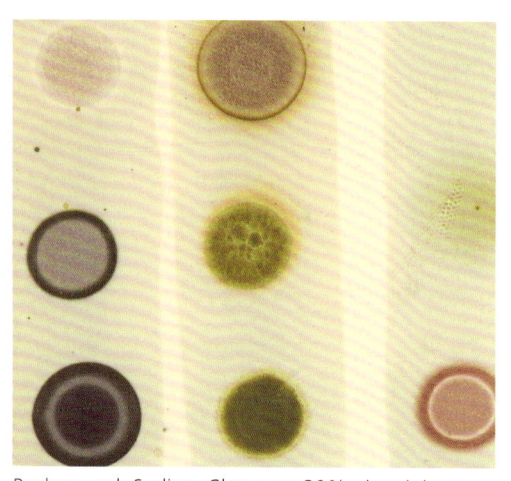

Background: Sodium Chromate 30% pinstriping tape resist.

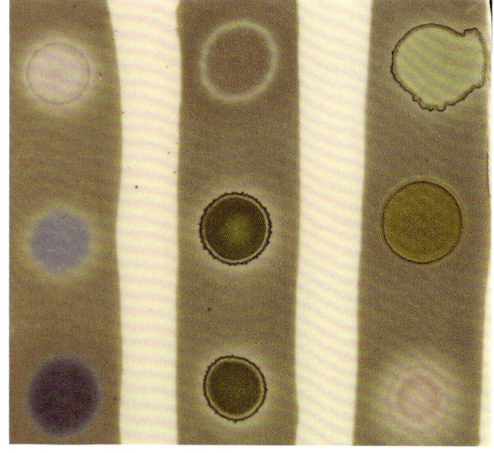

Background: Vanadyl Sulfate

135

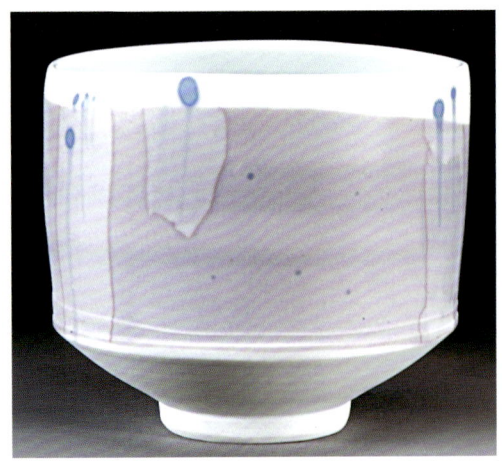

Glazing Techniques

After latex resist was applied to the lip and underside of the bowl, a 2% gold chloride solution was painted around the entire bowl and a 50% tin chloride solution was painted in broad vertical strokes. The latex was removed and a 15% cobalt chloride solution was painted in dots and stripes on the inside and outside of the vessel.

Latex resist was painted on the lip and underside of the bowl. A 15% cobalt chloride solution, a 50% cobalt chloride solution and a 50% tungsten solution (with a small amount of sodium hydroxide to help dissolve the salts) were applied with an eye dropper onto the surface of the bowl. Phosphoric acid was added with an eye dropper to create halos by "removing" the central area of a previously painted color.

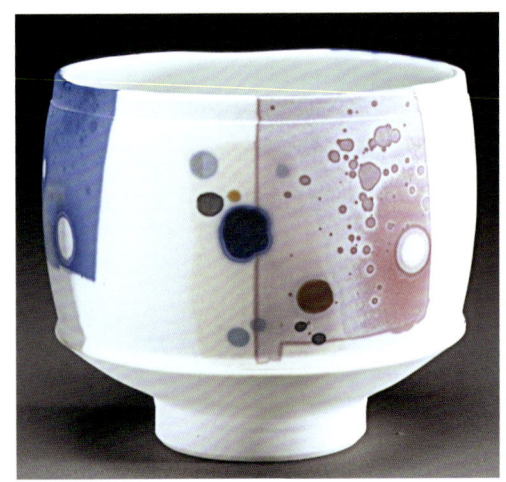

Latex resist was used to mask two rectangular areas before applying salts. On the left, a 50% cobalt chloride solution was painted on. Then phosphoric acid was added to create dots. On the right, a 2% gold chloride solution was painted on. A 50% tin chloride solution was dotted on with a brush. A second bisque firing was done to set the colors. Then a 30% vanadyl sulfate solution was painted on the left and 15% iron chloride was painted on the right. Separate solutions of 15% cobalt chloride, 50% cobalt chloride and 50% nickel were dotted on with an eye dropper.

COLOR	WATER-SOLUBLE METAL SALTS
gray	copper chloride (heavy application and heavy reduction can give pinks and reds) palladium chloride ruthenium chloride selenium (selenous acid, selenium toner) silver nitrate tellurium chloride vanadium (vanadyl sulfate, vanadium pentoxide)
blue	cobalt chloride molybdenum (molybdic acid)
green	ammonium chromate nickel chloride potassium dichromate sodium chromate
brown	iron chloride (iron chloride emits heat when mixed with water so the water should be added gradually in small amounts)
pink/ purple/ maroon	gold chloride (1–5% solution, adding either cobalt, manganese or tellurium will give different shades)
yellow	praseodymium chloride (very pale color)
black	cobalt chloride (50% solution) and iron chloride (100% solution) cobalt chloride (50% solution) and nickel chloride (50% solution) NOTE: neither of these combinations will yield a true black, just a close approximation.

WARNING

These materials are toxic in the raw stage. You must read and understand all safety precautions on the previous pages before using these materials.